SWITCHER STRIKES

OMAR ZAHID'S

*Eternal thanks to all collaborators on this collection of short stories.
God bless you all.*

Editors & Reviewers: Lindsy Moon, Nicky Frank, Emma Deas, Owen Sage, Drypaint, Hamza Alishah

Publisher: Maxmilian Nemec - TANEZCOR

Illustrations: Pepigrind, Lisa Kisaz, Dhidik Prasetio

Cover Illustration: Pepigrind

Cover Design: Laxlucifer

Book Design: Global Design

Copyright: Maxmilian Nemec

Company: Tanezcor Pictures LLC, Tanezcor Film Productions, Maxmilian Nemec - TANEZCOR & International Investors

ISBN: 978-80-908692-0-2

Only fools are in a hurry…

A TABLE OF CONTENT

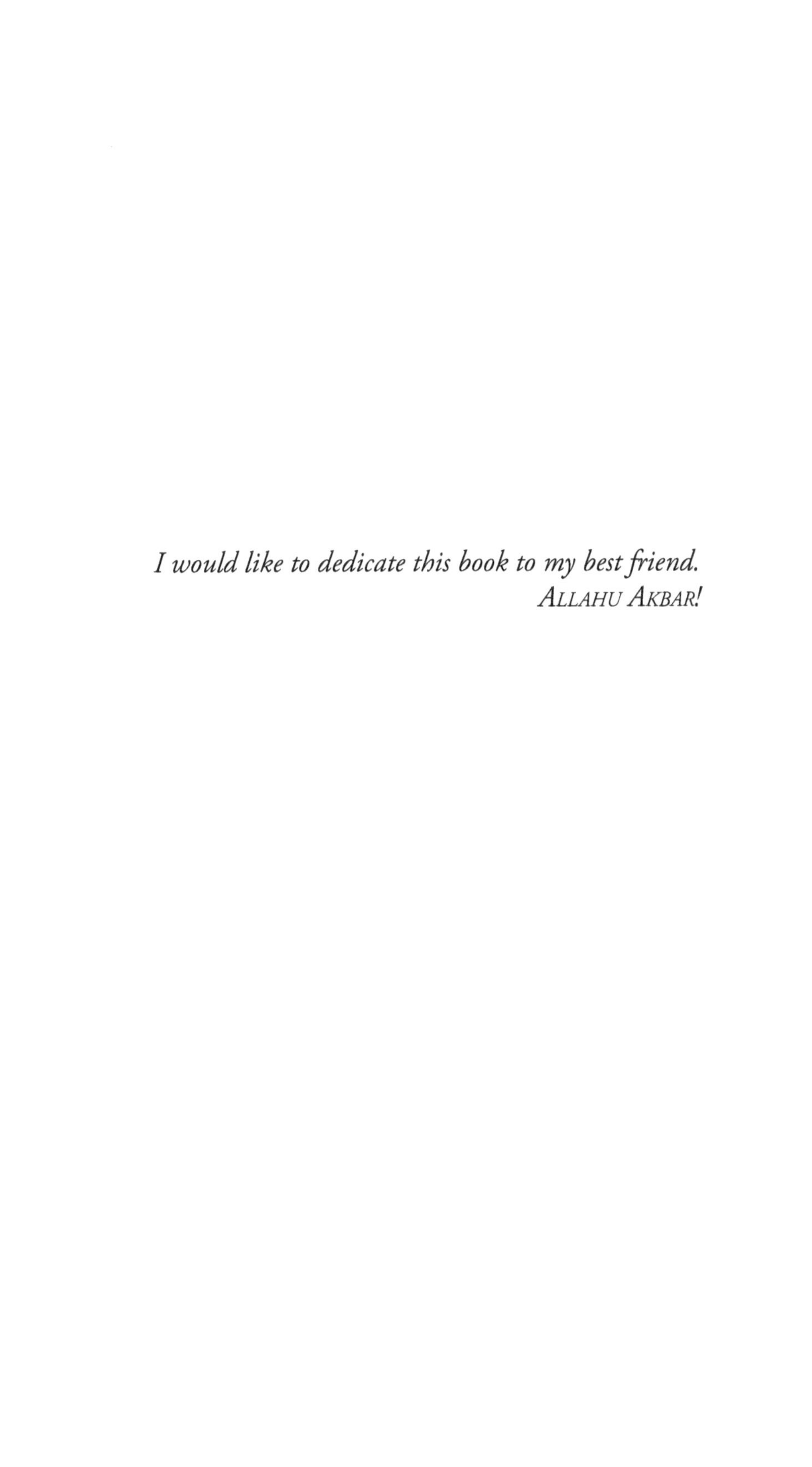

I would like to dedicate this book to my best friend.
ALLAHU AKBAR!

LAST CALL: PLANE TO ANTARCTICA

Another shitty day at the office. Not because of boring investor meetings with people twice my age, stacks of paperwork to read and sign, or the endless complaints dumb clients mail in. I dealt with that and more for eight hours each day, but no, today was far worse than anything I and every other person on this planet could have imagined possible: history repeating itself for the third time.

Laureate Tower, one of my family's properties down at Bellwood and head office of Winner Industries. I never had any problems getting to work on time, but these military checkpoints caused traffic all over Chicago.

"Alan, dear. I know you're a busy man but don't skip lunch, okay?"

I was talking to my mom on the phone as my driver dropped me off. She'd call me everywhere I went. It may seem overprotective, but I was all she had left.

"Yes, mom."

"Did you bring your vitamins? An extra shirt?"

"Yes, and yes. Don't worry. I'll call you later. Love you. Bye."

"Wait. One last thing. Come home early." She said, dropping her clingy tone. "I heard... a rumour from one of our clients. Something could happen today."

"Okay. No problem." As I reached the elevator, a familiar face was inside carrying a lot of documents in her suitcase. I caught myself staring at the spark in her eyes for too long.

She overheard a part of our conversation. Faking her surprise, she said. "Well, look who it is. Mommy's precious little baby Ally."

Mom heard everything through my phone. "Is that Silvestra? What is she doing there?

Take the next elevator, dear. She's a bad influence. I don't want you getting anywhere near her." I saw a crowd piling up by the entrance. Dozens of people hoped to clock in before their shift started. I'd rather step inside than deal with the morning rush.

She closed it as soon as I got in. We were by ourselves in the elevator. I would never grow tired of the Dior perfume she loved so much. If only I wasn't such a coward.

Silvestra laughed. "What's this? Alan lying to his mom? Oh my. I thought you haven't changed after all these years."

"I-It's just better to be here with y-you than to be late. Mom wouldn't like that." I looked away from her. My flushed cheeks in the reflection. I couldn't be any more obvious than this.

"It's always mom this and mom that with you. Do you ever think for yourself?"

"Of course! I make my own choices. My life doesn't revolve around her."

She stayed silent for the rest of the ride. I wasn't the type to loose my composure.

"Ah, here's my stop. Wouldn't want to take more of your time, seeing as you're such a busy man now." She said, pointing at the fifth floor. "Nice choice of words, Alan. Why didn't you say that back then?"

"What do you..."

As the elevator closed, she said. "I just wanted you to fight for me."

My office was on the thirtieth floor. The top floor. A clear view of the city reaching all the way to the fields of Indiana.

"Good morning, Mr. Winner." My secretary greeted me. When I was younger, she'd be referring to dad. But here I am, CEO at 25. Hearing it was a reminder that he's gone.

Mornings were the slowest part of my day. I opened a drawer with a worn out bracelet and a picture frame. Two kids without a care in the world. Back when Silvestra and I were inseparable. Anyone who saw us would think we were a couple. I wanted us to be, but I ruined any chance of that.

I saw my employees running past my door. They were gathering at a window by my office. It was too early for them to take a break. "Is that?" One man said.

"I think so." Replied another.

An old woman puts on her glasses. "I-I'm not seeing things, right?"

"IT'S HERE! IT'S HERE! RUN!"

What's here? I turned around and a speck in the distance was falling from the sky, hurling towards Indianapolis. That... that couldn't be what I thought it was.

Air raid sirens confirmed our fears. None of us had ever heard it before, but we all knew what it meant. The modern day drums of war.

I was frozen. Hands shaking. My heart, desperately slamming my chest. Mom, what now?

The speck, no... bomb erupted into a cloud with a deafening roar. The skies bled from a flash of light painting it in white, then crimson. The rumbling fissures were telling me to move. While they all ran, I reached for my phone. Silvestra was right. I never changed. I was always a scared little kid who couldn't do anything without his mom's approval. Even now, as death called me home.

My whole body felt like I was thrown into a wall. Ears ringing. A stinging pain pounding on my temples. No broken bones. Some bruises, light scratches here and there. The air didn't feel any different. No radiation so far.

I was... alive. How long was I out?

Debris filled my office. My perfect view of the horizon was smoke and ash, hiding the sun in shame for what humanity has done once more. Fires in every street as far as I could see. Cars, trees and bodies flung into the red river. The whole city was in chaos.

Something was making noise under rubble. It was... my ringtone. Mom was calling. "Alan? Alan! Oh, thank God my baby's alright. I've been trying to call you for hours." "What... happened here?"

"It's hard to take in but... it's starting. The third world war. Our friends in the east have gone crazy, calling in nukes all across the world. But it's okay, dear. Now that I've confirmed you're alive, I can ask for a chopper to pick you up."

"Pick me up? Where are you?"

"O'Hare Airport. The UN's prepared for this, as depressing as that sounds. We're taking our plane to Antarctica. Get to the rooftop. I'll call you soon."

Our plane had more than enough space for everyone here to come along. I went to the main hall to tell them the good news. That is, if it was good news for any of them. Limbs and corpses scattered between rubble. Blood and guts on every corner. Those who survived the shockwave had no chance of moving from where they stood. It was a massacre. None of them were making it out of here.

"Mr... Winner..." My secretary said, her hips below buried under her desk.

"I got you. Is there anyone else out there? We need help!" I dragged her to the first aid kit by the stairs. As I was preparing to bandage her wounds, I realised she was lighter than I thought she'd be. She left a trail of blood leading to where I found her.

I threw up. The nauseating stench of rotting flesh. Everyone I've worked with these past few years, lifeless before my eyes. I couldn't take it. Why... Why was I the only one left unscathed? They deserved to live as much as I did. There had to be someone, anyone here I could save. Fuck!

Whirring blades were getting louder. Rescue has arrived at the rooftop. I called my mom as soon as it landed.

"Is he there? Oh, please get here quick, dear. The plane's ready to leave. Are you hungry? Thirsty? I-I can fix you a snack before you arrive."

"After what I just saw? I'm not in the mood for eating anything, mom. They're all-" I stopped in front of the chopper. Silvestra was still down there. How could I forget about her?

"What's wrong, dear?"

"Hey, mister. Can you wait a bit longer?"

"No can do, kid. I got places to go after you." The pilot said.

"Alan?" Mom asked. "If you forgot something, we can buy another once the war's over." "It's not that. I need to check on someone."

"Who are you... Whatever it is, there's no time."

"I can't, mom. Look, I just need-"

"One hour."

"What?"

"One hour. That's how much time we have left. They're dropping another bomb here. In this city. Please, Alan."

It was a ten minute drive to the airport from here. Fifty minutes to find her, and I had no way to know if she was still alive. I needed to find her. See what happened to her.

"Mom, I promise I'll get there. I'm sorry." I dropped the call without hearing her reply. "You sure about this, kid?"

I nodded. I wouldn't be able to rest with these thoughts at the back of my mind.

"Alright. Give us a call when you've found your girlfriend. I'll try to come back for you." "She's not my... How did you know?"

The pilot laughed, and gave me a thumbs up. "Why else would you stay behind? Good luck."

The chopper flew off into the suburbs. Did I regret this? Maybe, but I've already decided I was heading down there. Twenty five floors. Shouldn't take more than twenty minutes to walk downstairs, or so I thought.

I nearly fell to my death rushing into the staircase. There was no spiralling path leading to the ground. Nearly every floor in sight had no platforms past the door. Every other path was the same. The ladder in the elevator shaft was intact, but what would I do if the elevator crashed into me? There was one other way down, and it had to be the worst option.

* * *

I raided the janitor's closet after looting the key off his body. Not much else I could use around here. I packed rubber gloves, tools and bandages into my satchel, along with whatever I could salvage from my office.

The only path left was through the main vent. I tied a fire extinguisher to the end of two hundred-foot hoses and threw it down the vent. That would take me down around twenty or so floors. It should be safe to use as rope. Better than tying dozens of clothes together.

There was hardly any room to breathe sliding down. Vibrations from my boots hitting metal echoed all the way to the bottom, which was too dark to see. At the end of the hose, I slowly shimmied my way to the fifth with my gloves. I heard a crackling noise from above as I was unscrewing the vent. The noises grew louder and higher pitched. In my panic, the screwdriver slipped from my hands. I was lucky to have some change in my pocket. A quarter saved my life seconds before a grate fell on my head.

And here I was. The fifth floor. Thirty minutes have passed since I was left behind. The ceiling was unstable. A lightbulb broke off, nearly hitting me. Puddles were leaking everywhere from the cafeteria above. This place was hit harder than the top. I remembered the way to Silvestra's office... from the time I followed her there. I wondered if she found out.

Her door was blocked by piles of rubble. Loose cables hung from above where her desk should be. I looked around, saying, "Silvestra? Are you there?"

"Alan? What are you doing here?" Her muffled voice said.

"I... umm... am here to save you."

"Don't bother. They all left me behind. I'm not hurt but I can't move from under this."

She was trapped under large slabs of concrete by the door. I pulled them off one by one, scratching my palms from tiny bumps on the surface. "Just get out of here, Alan!"

"No! Shut up and wait for me." I gasped. This was too tiring for a lanky executive. "I'm not leaving you again."

After some time, two more slabs were left. Bigger than the rest. "Are you still there?" She didn't reply. Was she injured? There wasn't any blood on the floor.

"Silv-"

"You told me to shut up!"

"Oh. I'm... almost... done here." My arms were exhausted. I continued, "One more and-"

The ceiling caved in on me. I crashed onto the floor below and broke a rib. I saw a piece of rebar fall onto me. I had no strength to dodge, so I pushed myself as far as I could from hitting anything vital. It pierced above the side of my hip, pinning me into the ground.

I heard sparks from behind Silvestra. The cables! If those reached anything flammable...Shit. Smoke was filling her office. I felt the heat from here.

"ALAN! Oh god. Please tell me you're still there."

"I'm... fine." I couldn't pass out. Not here. Not now. My vision was starting to blur. My left arm wouldn't move. Was this it for us?

I... needed to get up. The world was spinning. To save her I had to... Ah, fuck it. Now or never, Alan. Be the hero she needed right now.

I took a deep breath. I bit my lips as I pulled the rebar out of the ground, scratching against my insides with each inch I moved it. I teared up, holding in the urge to scream. The pain was too much for me to bear, yet when I thought of Silvestra, it was enough to give me the will to keep going.

I climbed up the rubble leading upstairs, with my torso still pierced through. Dripping blood down the rusty iron bar. The final slab blocking my way was scorching hot. That didn't matter.

"You're... safe now." My hands were burned. I was losing my balance.

Silvestra caught me as I stumbled onto her. She pulled us away, saying, "I got you." "My bag... there's... bandages inside."

I tried to pull out the rebar, but she shoved my hands away.

"You dumbass. It's not like the movies! You'll die if you do that. I... " She hugged me. My shoulder was soaked in tears. "I can't let that happen."

I placed my hand behind her head. "I'm sorry."

"You don't have to be."

"No, not that. For... what I did that day. My mom's a huge part of me, and you are too." "You didn't say anything when she blamed me."

"I know. My whole life I thought my mom was always right. I couldn't disappoint her, but losing you felt even worse."

"Then... you'll have to make up for all those years. I don't suppose you have a plan to get us out, do you?"

"Right here." I showed her my phone. It was split in half after the fall. "No... No. No. No. Give me your phone."

"Can't. Battery's dead." She said, tapping the power button.

"If I can't call our ride back, I don't know how we'll make it."

Silvestra brought out keys. "Unlike you, I have to drive here. My car's in the basement." An old sedan. A hand-me-down from her father. The windows were shattered, as were the windows on every other car. She was circling it to inspect each part. Leaning on the door, I said. "Come on. We gotta move."

"Who owns the car?"

"You do."

"Do you even know how to drive?"

I sighed. "No."

"Then stop complaining and let me see if this thing even works."

A car crash was blocking the ramp. Two SUVs. By the looks of it, they were abandoned not long ago.

"Hold on." She stepped on the gas, ramming through the roadblock.

I kept my hand pressed down on my stomach. "Do you always drive like this?"

"You told me to rush. It's not everyday I'm driving for my life." She glanced at my bloody hand. "How long do we have?"

I could barely read the time on the dashboard. "Twelve minutes."

"Hey, you've done enough already. Don't want you passing out in front of your mom."

My eyes were too heavy to keep them open. I've done more exercise today than I have in the past year. The streets were empty. There was nothing left to stop us now. "I'll... rest a bit."

"Alan? Wake up. We're here." Silvestra said, tapping my shoulder. "And three minutes to spare."

Silvestra helped me out of the car. The airport was nearly empty, save for mom's plane. Mom ran out as soon as she saw us.

"Alan! And... you." She slapped Silvestra. "I can't believe you would put him in danger. Look at him!"

"What? But he-"

"I knew you were trouble the moment I saw you. Poisoning his mind with your idea of fun. Lying. Sneaking out. Alan never disobeyed me before you showed up. I thought I told you to stay away from my boy. He's hurt because of you! Do you know how dangerous this place is?"

"I didn't ask him to-"

"You manipulated him! Nothing else makes sense. You know what, I should leave you here to die. Alan would-"

"MOTHER. STOP IT!" I screamed. Mom was shocked. "It was my idea to sneak out to the arcade back then. We've been hanging out for years before you caught us. And today... I chose to save her. I know you just want to protect me. All the time. But... you don't have to. I'm not your little Ally anymore. Let me do something on my own."

"I'm sorry. I try to guide you to what's best for you, but I was scared of letting you go. And Silvestra," She turned to face Silvestra. "I should've let you kids be free. I was the one holding him back."

We've left the city behind, along with the past we've let go. Silvestra called her family after charging her phone. They were on their way to Antarctica, just like us.

I waited for her call to end. "Hey, you forgot something."

"Oh my god. Did I leave something in the car?" She scrambled for her bag.

"No. Remember this?" I gave her the old bracelet I kept under my desk.

"I thought you threw that away?"

"Why would I? I was... hoping we'd go back to how we were someday. Or... umm... "

Taking a seat next to her, I continued. "Maybe more than how we were, Silvie."

"Hmm... What's that supposed to mean?"

"You know what I mean! Stop teasing me. J-just try it on."

The bracelet snapped halfway through her hand. We laughed it off. Of course it wouldn't fit. We were thirteen back then.

* * *

Though our everyday lives and countless people we knew we're now gone, what matters was that we were still here to keep moving forward and remember them by. Once the storm calmed down someday, I hoped that was the end of it. That humanity finally learned its lesson. That we could rebuild, and never again have to experience this tragedy.

There were no victors in war. Only those who lost, and those who lost more.

BEACH TOWN GEORGE

As he drove his rusty brown 1994 Chevrolet through Beach Town, George could not help but feel the silence that lurked within the bones of the small village. It was as though every single building, tree, person, and animal waited with bated breath for an unprecedented event. But nothing was ever going to happen, George knew this. Just as he felt, with every fibre of his being, that he would leave this world without even so much as a whisper in his life.

The gurgling chortle of his engine shattered the stillness in the streets as he drove along. Some of the villagers turned to look at the invader, their faces as calm and uncharacteristic as the Lake Michigan on a peaceful day, but their eyes – their eyes carried an ethereal aura. George felt the questioning in their eyes, the uncertainty. It was as harsh as the rays of the setting sun filtering in through the windshield and stabbing at his eyes.

He pulled the sun visor down and eased his foot into the gas.

A group of turkeys hollered and scattered as George's Chevrolet drove them from the entrance to his farmhouse. He put the truck to a stop right in front and stepped out quietly. George was not what most would call a striking man. He was 5 foot 5, had a bald crown, and a type of solemn sadness that sat on his wrinkled skin. Every step he took, every gesture, seemed to come from a place of defeat. The most illustrious moments of his life had been the 45 years he'd spent in the police force.

Now, he'd retired, and he'd sunk deep into oblivion, so much so that he couldn't recognize himself sometimes.

He walked over to the other side of the truck, a slight limp in his gait, and brought out the bags of fish he'd bought from the market.

As he walked inside, he was hit by a sudden gust of wind, almost as if an unseen force had spat a projectile of air at him. George spun around immediately, his knuckles white to the bone as he clutched the bags of fish tightly. There was a howl in the air as the wind combed through the land. George stared around, half in fright, and half in surprise. Then he turned, walked inside, and shut the door behind him. He did not see the drift of sand growing at the foot of his door until it turned into the form of a hooded figure. Just as quickly as it'd formed, the figure of dust degenerated and flew out with the wind.

Later that night, George sat in front of his TV, watching the news as the anchor predicted a hurricane in some parts of Illinois. The anchor was a young man, who dazzled in a shiny brown two-piece, slicked hair, and a confident smile.

You just wait, George thought. *You'll become like me soon enough. The world will forget you, and all your service and it'll be like you never existed.*

He cut some boiled fish with his knife, stuck it in his mouth and chewed. George could not tell how long it had gone on for, but slowly it dawned on him – the tapping sound on the window. It was like a knock, only lighter. George stared wide-eyed as he listened to the tapping. It went one, two, three, stopped, then continued again. He turned around and stared at the curtain. It undulated as the wind from outside beat on it, but the rhythm of the tapping on the window did not match the ferocity of the wind.

George gulped noisily. Then he reached for the Marlin 336C lying against the couch, cocked it and aimed it straight at the window as he approached. The undulations on the curtain increased until it felt like it was shivering from a cold. George's heart raced, and he felt the air in the room tighten until it was hard to breathe. A howl began to grow behind the curtains as they writhed around. George stretched an arm tentatively, while the other held the gun. In a temporary flare of courage, he swiped the curtain aside, yelling, and ready to fire.

But he was met with nothing. Nothing at all, but an endless sprawl of night and very bad weather. His face was a mask of pure relief as his palpitating heart slowed. He stared out into the night. Flashes of lightning broke out intermittently from underneath thick pillows of furious clouds, breaking the hold of darkness on the land. But it was only momentarily, and after that bright spike, darkness would cover the entire place again.

"All this bad weather," George muttered before pulling his head back in. He shut the window. Then shut all other windows keeping the fury of the wind outside.

The broadcast on the TV was breaking up now, but George could still make out a couple of words from the anchor.

"Please…indoors…hurricane…largest…"

George trudged over to the TV and pulled the plug.

"No one's stupid enough to go out in this kind of weather anyways," he thought out loud. He finished up his dinner, took the plates out and went to bed.

* * *

"Hello!" George yelled. "Is anyone out there!"

He got no response. Nothing, but the shriek of the wind.

He held up his arm as he tried to keep the revolving pillar of sand from entering his narrowed eyes. *I could swear I'd seen someone right in the storm,* he thought. He turned around, trying to make sense of his surroundings, but it looked like he was trapped within a giant castle of flowing sand.

Suddenly, George stifled. He thought he'd heard someone call his name from within the storm.

"Is someone there!" he called out again. "Stop playing games with me! I'm an ex-cop. Trust me, I'm not someone you want to be messing with!"

George stared into the storm for a while, but he got nothing. It was just a storm. Suddenly, everything stopped. It was all quiet. Like all the sound had been sucked from the world. George turned, and almost bumped into a face in the storm.

"Jesus Christ!" George screamed as he blanched.

His skin turned white as he stared, horrified, at the grinning face made of sand.

"Hey, George. I'm glad you came back."

"Who...Who...who..." George's lips quivered as he tried to speak.

"Who am I?" the face asked.

It detached itself from the wall of sand, floating momentarily. A stream of sand flowed from the wall, attaching itself to the face, forming a definite shape, until a tall man in a long cloak stood right in front of George.

"O, God, where am I? George asked, stupefied.

"Guess," the man said. "Where are you?"

"I'm dead, right? This is the afterlife, isn't it?"

"No George, you're only dreaming."

George sighed audibly. The relief he felt was tremendous. *I'm going to wake up soon,* he thought.

"It's laughable."

"What is?" George asked.

"The relief on your face. You think this is a figment of imagination, but it isn't."

"What is it then?"

"A reunion. The continuation of where we left off years ago."

"Where did you leave off? What reunion?"

"You'll know soon enough."

"Wait, what?"

George's eyes flipped open, and he sat up with an audible gasp. He looked around, searching for the stranger in his dreams, but he was confronted by the familiarity of his bedroom. His shoulders dropped as he bowed his head, relieved that he'd finally woken up.

"That was weird," he said out loud. He shook his head, got out of bed, and got into the bathroom. He splashed some water on his face and stared into the mirror.

"You're an old man, George," he said. "An old man struggling with the fact his life is coming to a close."

After a while of staring, he shook his head, and left for the living room.

George knew something was wrong the moment he felt the cold wet air on his face. He looked up and saw leaves, dirt, and broken branches strewn across the living room. The door was wide open.

"What the hell!" George frowned as he stepped closer. He was growing old, but he could remember clearly that the door had been firmly shut. George flung his eyes around, trying to check if this was a break in. His hunting rifle was still there; the rest of his stuff too. He walked out onto the porch and looked at the last spot he'd parked his truck. It was still there. This was no break in. There was no break in at all.

He stretched his eyes further out into the open. It looked like giants had staged a heated fight through the entire place. Trees had been uprooted, the sturdier ones had their branches snapped, the grasses were matted hard against the ground. The storm hadn't even spared the barn. There were holes on its roof from where sheets of zinc had been ripped off.

George turned and walked back in, wondering when the disaster the weather had wreaked would be fixed. Suddenly, his eyes fell on a package sitting right beside the couch. He hadn't seen it when he walked out because it was facing the door.

He narrowed his eyes, and the wrinkles on his face deepened. The package, whatever it was, wasn't there last night. He looked around the room again, more cautiously this time. It was as if he was expecting someone to jump out and yell "surprise!"

He stepped closer, getting a good look at the box.

It was a metal detector. More wrinkles grew on George's face. Why would anyone drop off a metal detector in his living room?

It was then that he saw it – sprinkles of dust on the package. But they weren't just sprinkles, George realised with a start. They were words.

Open up, Georgie!

He looked around. *Is this a prank?* He thought. It had to be.

He got down on his knees and unboxed the metal detector. It was brand new. The leaves in the living room rustled as a slow breeze floated in through the open door. George turned around, and pulled his head back instantly. He thought the leaves were moving quite unnaturally, until his eyes widened. They had just formed new words.

The back. Now!

George was many things. Confused, frightened, nervous. But he was a cop, and that desire to always follow things up was not something he could shake off in a blink. Holding the metal detector, he went out to the back of the house. The hurricane had not spared it either, and there were loose clumps of soil from where shrubs had been ripped out.

The metal detector beeped as it came to life, and George flinched, nearly dropping it. He stared at the device, confusion swimming in his eyes. He hadn't put it on, but he had not been doing anything himself since morning either. He stared at the metal detector again. It went off. Then it came on.

George stared at it, convinced it was broken as it repeated the same on and off motion. But then he took a step, and it steadied. He paused, his eyes distant as thoughts rolled through his mind. He knew what he had to do now. He held the detector close to the ground, and he moved forward.

George was nearing the end of the yard when the detector beeped excitedly. It had picked up something. His eyes narrowed as he peered at the spot. There was something there, a raised patch of earth. No. He stopped closer. There was more. He swiped the earth off with his hand, revealing a rusted metal box.

He cocked his brow. Immediately, he let the detector go. He got to his knees, and used his fingers to free the box from the soil around it.

Freeing the box was easier than George had thought; though his shoulders heaved when he was done. He lifted the box, and cocked his brow. It was surprisingly light. Thankfully, the lid was not locked. George placed it on the ground and opened it.

The excitement drained from his face instantly, and was replaced with profound disappointment. A neatly folded orange handkerchief sat in the middle of the box. George didn't know how long it had been buried, but for the few spots of rust on it, the handkerchief looked to be in perfect condition.

George stuck his hand in and picked the handkerchief. The longer he stared at it, the deeper he frowned. There was something acutely familiar about it. And then, from out of the blue, it hit him – a memory so distant it could have as well been in monochrome colours. He saw a girl giggling and running around the house with her new possession – an orange-handkerchief a gypsy gifted her. That was his sister. A week later, she would disappear without a trace, and never be found again.

George got to his feet, holding the handkerchief like a piece of evidence. What was it doing here? After decades?

Suddenly, George winced as his head was filled with a rush of voices. His hand involuntarily formed a fist around the handkerchief, and the voices climbed, shattering the sanctity of his mind like an invasion. He groaned as he staggered and fell on his knees. He bowled his fists until his knuckles turned white. The voices reached a crescendo and then they stopped abruptly. George's groaning and grimace stopped in a like manner. He got to his feet with tight fists and a face drained entirely of emotion. His eyes looked distant, lost.

He walked into the house, out the front door, and made his way towards Lake Michigan.

That was the last anyone ever saw or heard from George.

People would talk about him afterwards. They'd found the metal detector lying in his backyard as well as a rusted box and the hole he'd freed it from. The story was old George had found gold and fled with it so no one would disturb him.

He'd come into Beach Town to leave the world quietly. He did leave quietly, but he left a tale on the tongues of villagers, and anyone who came in, would hear of the tale of Beach Town George.

WHAT HAPPENED TO ALEX KINDER

had always known that my relationships could make or mar me. This is why from high school down to college I was very picky with friends. I was the life of the party, the one everyone wanted as a friend but I carefully chose those who got to know me, I mean the real me. One of those friends was Pascal Dandy. I met Pascal as a freshman in college, we had some courses together and a particular day when I was late to class he scooted and waved me over

"Thank you so much," I said

"Don't mention it"

By the end of the class, we were fast buddies, we had spent most of the class discussing our interests because the course was abstract and the class was boring.

"It's nice to meet you, Alex"

"Same here, it's been a long time since I had a long and meaningful conversation with anybody. You have such an intelligent mind and you talk of business as if you had gone to a business school"

"Well" he touched his hair "my family was not particularly well off when we were children but my dad always bought books. I didn't spend so much time with the TV so I read a lot of books especially business books because they fascinate me"

"Have you been able to practise what you learned?"

"If a lemonade stall in middle school counts, then yes. If not, then no."

I laughed loudly "Trust me, it does, you are a lot better than I am. I have never started anything business related. Even though I have a lot of interest in it" I whispered to him "I plan to own a very large corporation in the future so that I can have enough money to live a cool life."

Pascal gave a wide smile "You dream big"

"Haven't you ever heard? If you are going to dream, ensure that it is big"

"True, what do you say? We continue this conversation at Lulu's cafe. I'm craving a hot cup of coffee and cinnamon rolls"

"Deal"

It was as if I had met the cool headed version of me, we thought alike and sometimes acted alike. The only difference was that he kept to himself more than I did. Pascal became the friend I shared all my secrets with, he knew about my life even before my family, my two younger brothers even got jealous at a point in our friendship. We were tagged best friends in college and it was true on my part. The only problem was that Pascal revealed so little about himself, he had met my family in college and knew almost everything about me but I knew so little about him. This caused me to be wary at first but during the course of our friendship, I dispelled my worries and chose to give my full trust to Pascal.

After leaving college, I went on to a business school while Pascal worked jobs in order to gain enough experience. Five years after college while having lunch together we brainstormed a business idea and decided to be partners. We started from a small office and in a few years, we had our own building and had spread all over America. What we did was simple, we sought unemployed people and connected them with companies that had vacancies. Sometimes we had to lobby for slots in the company. My time in the company was usually spent discussing with Alex on how to move our business forward. While approaching his office one day, I could hear distinct voices.

"Mr. Chandler does not plan to use his shares in the company to support our agenda. In fact, in tomorrow's board meeting he has plans to vote against us" Sandra (Alex's personal secretary) said.

"What?" Alex's voice was raised "I thought we had given him enough bribes to make sure he's on our size"

"He's definitely not enough"

"If he doesn't change his mind before tomorrow's meeting then ensure you stop him from coming for the meeting. Even if you have to cause an accident, it must be done. Mr. Chandler must not be around"

"Just like you scheduled Miss Riley would be the one to kickstart our agenda"

I was not aware of any agenda, in fact, I had barely been told about the meeting. Was Alex trying to cheat me? Was he trying to go do things behind my back? At that moment I became suspicious of Pascal. It looked as if Alex had a lot of underground activities that he was acting out. The meeting the next day went exactly how Pascal had said, it was making more sense to me that it was staged. I pulled Pascal aside after the meeting "Pascal, do you remember how many years we have been together? Remember how we met and how we started this company?"

"Yes I do," he said with a fond smile "The best decision in my life was to talk with you that day"

I smiled "How is your wife?"

"Still bossy and stubborn as usual"

"Pascal I won't lie to you, I do not like anything underhanded. Why have you been meeting shareholders behind my back? What is your plan?"

His eyes widened a fraction "It's not what you think. I have been seeking the support of the shareholders in case some big happened again"

I wanted to believe Pascal, I really wanted to but all facts showed me that he was acting strange. I tried not to think about it but my mind was really worried. Pascal had more influence in the company because of his business acumen, but I had been pushed to the side for many years. In spite of this, I was still the largest shareholder at A and P cooperation. My phone began to ring, the call was from Suzy, my personal assistant. What again? I wondered.

"Good evening sir"

"Good evening Suzy"

"I have a quick report to give you, Mr. Pascal has been secretly meeting with the other shareholders for many months now and I did not bother you with this information because I wanted to speak when I had more facts. I have just heard that the purpose of his secret meetings has been to find a way to oust you from A and P cooperation"

My mind went blank. No, Pascal will not do that, not after many years of friendship.

"Mr. Alex, Mr. Alex…"

"Do you have evidence or any form of proof of the accusation you are making?"

"Not yet sir"

"Do not make such damaging statements without adequate proof"

"Alright sir"

"Thank you for your concern but I trust Pascal"

I had finally arrived at home, the house was eerily quiet. Living alone was not as easy as I thought. I untied my tie and sat on the chair in my dining room while rubbing my forehead. I had developed a sudden headache after the call with Suzy. Pascal could not have tried to harm me, there must be a different explanation to what is going on. I had taken money from my family in order to start A and P cooperation, my mom and dad barely believed in the company but still invested because of me. Automatically, I was the highest investor and I had the largest shares. There would be no A and P cooperation without my contribution. Input my hand through my brown hair. The thought of Pascal harming me became so bothersome that I decided to visit Pascal at home to clarify what was going on. The drive to his place was a short one, we had chosen our houses together and considered the distance.

I pressed the doorbell and waited for a response. Pascal opened the door with a surprised look on his face "Look who we have here, honey, Alex is here"

I smiled and stepped into the house. Their house was small but tastefully furnished. Patrick, their son ran to hug me immediately he heard my name.

"Uncle Pascal, it has been long since I saw you"

"Yes, it has bud" I spent the whole time at his house avoiding the topic that was burning in my heart. I quickly used the restroom in his house and on my way out I stumbled on the conversation between Pascal and his wife.

"What is he doing here?"

"I didn't know he was coming and so I could not tell you. I also was not aware he was coming. "

"I already told you I do not like that man. You guys may have been friends but he lets you do bulk of the work and still gets well paid"

"Babe" he held on to her hand, "I told you I am already working on it. Very soon he won't be part of the company. His time there is limited"

I hid and came out only after they left. Suzy was not lying, she had been telling the truth. I only believed what I wanted to because of my friendship. I quickly departed from their home after that claiming an upset stomach. I was still struggling with believing it. Pascal was that friend when I had no one. Why was he doing this to me? Why was he picking the business over our friendship?

I went home strategizing on what to do. I placed a quick call to my mom, she was the business expert in my family who had started up a company whose net worth was in millions of dollars.

"Hi, mom"

"Alex...to what do I owe the honour of this phone call," she said in a teasing tone.

"Come on, mom. I'm not that bad. I call at least twice a week."

"Is that enough? Is that how many times you should call the mother who raised you"

"Alright, I'm sorry mom but you know work can be consuming"

"What is wrong?"

"Why do you think something is wrong?"

"Well, your voice quivered when you mentioned work? Tell me what is going on and do not lie to me, Alex"

"You know me too well"

"I'm your mother"

"Let me go straight to the point then. Pascal is trying to kick me out of the company by getting the shareholder's votes"

"What?!!! I told you that that boy was a gold digger but you did not believe me. After all the money we invested and after all the time we have put in, he wants to kick you out. I will destroy him myself"

"Mom, this is not the time to be emotional. I called to ask for your advice. What do you think I should do?"

"Alex, fight back with everything you've got. Don't try to step down for him. If he is trying to kick you out then he must not have it easy. Talk to the shareholders, they should be able to do something"

"Alright mom, thanks for the advice"

"Let me know how it goes"

"Sure thing, bye mom"

"Bye"

If Pascal could get the right number of votes, he could oust me from the company. I called all the shareholders I had on my contact list and scheduled a meeting with them. I would keep my place in the company no matter the cost. It was shocking to me to see what Pascal was doing but I could not say I had no hints over the years. My family warned me about him for so many years till I kept a distance from them because of my friendship with Pascal. I noticed he acted a little jealous of my background because I grew up with rich parents while he grew up in a poor environment. I had seen many signals but ignored them because I chose to believe the best of my friend.

A wave of uncharacteristic anger came over me and I wanted to destroy Pascal. I decided to sleep it off and make no hasty decisions. The next day I focused on meeting with the shareholders. I spent time convincing them that I had their best interest at heart and not Pascal. By the time I would return to the office, I was exhausted and tried to rest in my chair. Pascal stepped in at that moment.

"Where have you been? It is unusual to not find you in your office"

"Oh, here and there"

He walked to the back of my seat but I kept my eyes closed. He was standing right behind me when I felt a syringe dig into the skin of my neck.

"What are you doing Pascal?" I said with alarm in my voice trying to struggle with him but he held me in place.

"I should ask you the same"

Whatever he had injected me with was kicking into my system. My eyes bulged as I struggled to breathe. I could not talk, I could not do anything.

"I always hated having to kiss up to you but that was my only ticket out of poverty. You thought we met by chance in college. Ha," he laughed "I orchestrated that meeting after hearing you were the richest guy on campus. You helped me start this company but you were not useful to it anyway. It is my company, I do not care how many hours you spent working here or how much money you invested in its start up, it was always meant to be Pascal's cooperation. I had planned to cause you to quit in peace but you just had to meet with the shareholders, didn't you? Well, if you would not leave the easy way you would the hard way"

I could not resist him, I could hear what he was saying but I felt as if I was paralyzed. His voice suddenly changed and he shouted in panic.

"Help, help, I don't know what is going on with Alex. He just suddenly slumped, he is no longer talking. Can someone call the ambulance?"

The noise of the siren of the ambulance was the next thing I heard. I fell into a deep sleep, it felt as if I was in a black hole. Pascal had ruined my life.

I opened my eyes and saw myself in a blue patient's gown. My body looked dry and cracked, I tried to stand but my legs were weak. I tried again and I could finally walk. What was going on? Where exactly am I?

Why am I in this gown? The flood of memories came back. I suddenly remembered what Pascal did to me and I was filled with anger. I walked around the hospital trying to find someone to talk to. I met a nurse and asked

"Hello, ma'am, please can you tell me what today's date is?"

"8th March 2026"

"What? That can't be right. 6 years have passed since I was admitted here. Was I in a coma?"

"No, you were not, you were one of our most active patients even though your words were not usually coherent"

"Wow" I've been awake but not awake. What does that mean? This is the first time I am regaining consciousness in 6 years but I have been walking and living. What exactly happened to me? I could not wait to figure it out. Within a few hours, I deduced I was in a mental hospital. This is what Pascal had done to me. Whatever he injected in my veins had stolen 6 years of my life from me. I needed to escape from this place. I studied the routine of the workers for a few days and decided that the only way out was to use a workers identity card and to wear their clothes.

On the day of my escape, I shaved my beards and prepared my mind to fight Pascal with everything I have to get back my place in A and P cooperation. I was already prepared in the early hours of the morning. By 7 am one of the workers arrived, the cleaner started work in my room. I pretended to be asleep before hitting his head and knocking him out. I quickly changed into his clothes and took his ID. I walked outside my room pushing his cleaning equipment and using it as a shield for my face. I made it to the automated door and used his ID to open the door. I was out of the facility within a few minutes. I could not believe my luck, I ran as fast as my legs could carry me without looking back trying to get as far away as possible from the clinic. Luckily, the psychiatric hospital was in the outskirts of my city, Maze city. I finally got to see residential houses when it was almost evening. As I walked through the city, I realised something was wrong. I could not place my finger on it but it seemed the changes in Maze city in the past 6 years were monumental. I walked around looking for the A and P building but the building seemed to have vanished. I began to wonder if I was in the right city. I walked around and saw a few people on the street. They all looked sickly with a strange yellow glow under their skin, even young children looked this way. What exactly was going on?

At the end of the street, a well-dressed man sat beside a stall. A great queue stood in front of his stall and people were pushing themselves in order to get a spot on the queue. I walked over fast wondering what the man could be selling. I was shocked to see syringes with green like substances displayed publicly as goods. He was selling drugs!

I walked up to him and held him by his shirt "You can't be doing this! How can you be selling drugs publicly? That is illegal"

"Hey, who are you? I got a permit before setting up my stall and it is one of the many stalls holding these goods. What right do you have to confront me here"

I did not know who landed the first punch but as the fight grew hotter, I felt someone drag me away forcefully. I could barely resist.

"Hey! Who are you? Let me go!" I shouted in fear. The man did not reply but kept dragging me till we got to a very old building. He held the door open, pulled me inside, and took me to the basement. I just escaped one prison for another. What is the point of regaining consciousness after 6 years for this? What exactly is wrong with Maze city?

"Who are you?" The man asked

"I think I am the one who should ask that question"

"Answer me first!"

"I am Alex Kinder"

"Why did you cause a scene?"

"Is it normal to have drugs sold in broad daylight?"

"Uh yeah it is, although we don't call them drugs, we call them lifelines"

"Lifelines, what exactly is going on? I lose consciousness for 6 years and everything turns upside down"

"You lost consciousness for 6 years?"

"Yes"

"What hospital were you in?"

"Mayday psychiatric hospital"

"Mayday" he rubbed his beard "That is where the big man keeps everyone he hates"

"The big man?" I was brimming with questions.

"Wait for a little, I'll explain what is going on. Two more people will be joining us."

Within a few minutes, the people he mentioned arrived. A lady with raven black hair and a leather jacket and jeans and a younger man with red hair, glasses, and a very serious face. I was curious about them and I sensed that they were about me.

"Let me start by introducing myself, my name is Adam and these two are my friends and colleagues"

What an unlikely group of friends. Adam looked like a refined boxer, the lady looked like a rockstar while the young guy looked like a regular geek.

"The lady's name is Asher while this my young friend is Peter"

"Uh, nice to meet you," I said

"Asher, Peter meet Alex" they nodded "Alright, so Alex the first thing you should know is that a lot has changed since you lost consciousness six years ago. The big man I referred to was Pascal, he usurped power and took over the government about four years ago. What you saw out there was the effect of his rule. He legalised drugs and began selling them to anyone willing to buy them, when he felt only a few people were purchasing his goods, he began adding them to the water system. Tap water was filled with drugs, distilled bottle water was also filled with drugs so that a young child is addicted before they are 5. The drugs were specially created to keep everyone under control. He has achieved that so far but some of us came together to form a resistance group. We are the leaders of the resistance group. We found a way to distil water ourselves so that we can stay clean from the drugs and we are trying to find a way to remove Pascal from the position of power."

"Wow, those are serious developments. Why are other cities not helping us?"

"The big man has great military power and a lot of money. Nobody is willing to go against him"

"That's crazy. Wait, something just clicked in my mind. Did you say his name was Pascal?"

"Yes"

"What is his surname?"

"Dandy" I had to laugh at that point because things were getting interesting

"I get that his name may be a bit funny but it's not that funny," Asher said and rolled her eyes

"Oh, I have my reasons for laughing because your big man is my friend turned arch enemy. He stole my company and injected me with a drug that made me lose consciousness for 6 years."

"Ah, I understand the laughter now."

"You know him well then," Adam said

"You can say that."

"Well, we recently found out that Pascal's laboratory has discovered an antidote to the addiction to lifelines and plans to sell them at an exorbitant price. The plan is to steal at least one sample and recreate it so we can distribute it to everyone in the city."

"Good plan"

"It is," Peter said, "the problem is that we have no idea where he could keep the antidotes and how we will get it."

"If I know anything about Pascal it is that he is full of greed and loves to boast"

"How is that helpful?" Asher said

"Let me finish speaking" I gave her a look. "If he has something that is supposed to bring him so much money, he will keep it where he can see it regularly. The place where he spends most of his time"

"That makes sense" Adam held my gaze "He spends most time in his office but how do we get through the security"

"We can go at night"

"Even though there would be no person there, the defence technology in that building alone is great"

"Can it be hacked?" Peter asked

"I guess"

"Then leave that to me. The rest of you can figure out how to get there and leave without a scratch."

"Ok, let's inform the rest of the resistance group about this. Alex, you will be coming with us"

"Me, but I just got out of the hospital, I have no training. I cannot even fight well"

"Do you want Pascal to continue to hurt people? Do you want to see children continue being addicted to drugs?"

"No"

"Then we need you with us."

"Alright."

We spent the day studying the map of Pascal's office. It was complex but we could figure out a way around it. Asher was still hostile to me, she drew Adam away. Although they tried to keep their voices down, I could hear them clearly.

"What if he was sent by Pascal?"

"He wasn't".

"How do you know? What if he is a spy? He could put the whole resistance movement at risk. We could die, Adam".

"We knew that when we decided to start a resistance group. If we cannot take a few risks then we may never succeed against Pascal. I trust my gut that guy is not a spy"

"I'll still keep an eye on him"

"Do as you wish"

I turned my eyes away as they joined us again. We finished planning and we prepared to leave.

"Are you going in that?" Peter asked. I was still dressed in the cleaner's uniform.

"That's all I have, right now"

"Get some clothes there," he said pointing to a box "and get changed to something black, we don't want you giving us away with that blue uniform"

"Oh, true, thanks Peter"

We left the basement and drove near Pascal's office in Adam's car. We waited a few hours for it to get dark while Peter worked his magic and hacked the security system of Pascal's office. When we felt it was dark enough, we snuck into the building leaving Peter in the car, the gate was locked so we had to jump over the fence. On getting inside the compound we looked around ensuring no security personnel were around. Once we entered the building, we walked carefully to ensure we did not set off any alarms. We had to get to the topmost floor through the stairs, Asher stayed behind me, watching me warily, still in doubt of my identity. The topmost floor was strangely still, almost as if something terrible was going to happen there.

"Have you disabled all alarms at the topmost floor, Peter?" Adam spoke into his mouthpiece

"Yes it's done"

Even with Peter's reassurance, we placed our feet carefully on the floor, anticipating any interruption. Peter unlocked the door to the office and we walked in. I was worried because everything seemed easy. Just too easy. We checked his drawers, checked everywhere in his office but did not find anything like the antidote.

Asher glared at me "I thought you said you knew him. The antidote is obviously not here. We risked our lives for nothing"

"This is not the time for that," Adam said angrily. I racked my brain, where could Pascal hide it in the office. Then I spotted his large family picture on the wall, I walked over to the wall and checked under the picture. I smiled in victory, under the picture was a safe

"Adam, Asher, there is a safe here. Come check it out"

They rushed over

"How do we get the password?" Adam said, hitting his head.

"Asher, type this number. It may be the birthday of his son"

That did not work

"Try his wife's birthday"

"His wedding anniversary"

"His birthday"

"They are all wrong," Avery said in frustration. The safe allowed only one more try before it would permanently lock.

What could his passcode be? What would make someone like Pascal happy?

"Try 08-03-20"

"What date is that?"

"The day he stole the cooperation from me and placed me in the psychiatric hospital"

Asher glanced at me for a minute before typing it in.

"It worked"

The safe opened and inside was what we were searching for. At least 50 vials of the antidote, we all smiled at each other. Asher packed them carefully into her backpack. Suddenly, the safe started making a loud beeping noise.

"What is going on?" Adam asked

"I don't know" replied Avery

I pushed them away and looked closely at the safe. It was requesting Pascal's fingerprint so it would not trigger a bomb to blow up the building.

"We are doomed"

"Asher, you need to get out of here first, climb down through the window and climb carefully. Those vials must not be broken"

She did as she was told

"Now what?" I said

"Keep trying your fingerprint to buy time for Asher"

"What will happen to us?"

"At the last minute, we will jump out"

I looked at him in horror, jumping out could possibly kill us. Staying inside would definitely kill us so we had no choice in the matter. At the last beep, Adam grabbed me and made a dive from the window. We fell into trees, I was hanging on one while Adam fell to the floor, he helped free my clothes from the tree and we ran out of the compound. We were barely in the car when the building blew. The impact shook Adam's car but we were still safe.

The next set of days was full of activities, Adam got his connection in a lab to develop more of the antidote and the other members of the resistance group ensured its distribution. By the end of the week, ninety percent of the people of Maze city had received the antidote. The second phase of the plan went into place. Peter hacked into the broadcasting station and played a video where Adam explained what Pascal had done to the citizens of Maze city to keep them under control. This led to mass protests and many crowded the front of Pascal's home. He fled the city at night with his family. Adam was elected as the new Governor of Maze city and we all met to discuss whether Adam should accept being Governor or not.

"I think you should go for it, Adam. You have the people's interest in mind" Asher said

"Honestly, I could not think of a better leader," I said and Peter nodded in agreement

"If I'll be taking up this position then I'll need you, people, with me, I cannot do it alone"

"Deal," we said. I had known Adam, Asher, and Peter for only a month but I realised what true friendship was like, it was nothing like what I had shared with Pascal who pretended to agree with everything I said in order to get me to like him. I argued with them but also came to a resolution with them. I stood to leave but could not help but tease Asher

"Do you now believe I am not Pascal's spy?"

"I think you will agree with me that it was reasonable doubt. You could have been his spy"

"But I was not."

"Alright. I agree I was wrong and I'm sorry" she said through her teeth.

"Oh, I didn't hear that"

"I said I'm sorry!" I grinned,

"I deserve a gift for my heroic deed despite your pessimistic attitude"

"Huh?"

I gave her my phone "Press in your number, I deserve a date"

She rolled her eyes "I don't date losers but this is a one-day exception"

I laughed, Asher would always be Asher.

A FOR ALPHA

The third day of the third month, I had not paid attention to it when many were discussing that something significant usually happens on dates that have recurring numbers. I wish I did, even if I had I would not have anticipated what happened. I am getting ahead of myself, let me explain why I could not have anticipated it. I was an ordinary factory worker trying to make ends meet, I was friendly but had few friends and on that day I had gone to work as usual. At about noon while I was taking a break a few feet from our factory, a bomb suddenly dropped close to the factory and a part of the factory caught fire. I was more than shocked, my country was not at war with any other country. We had maintained a state of peace for many years and avoided conflict due to our small size. I could not have imagined a bomb blast in my wildest dream. Although my mind was shocked, my body had moved into action joining the few factory members who were outside with me to try to save our colleagues who were in the factory during the bomb blast. It was not an easy task but it was one that caused many to call me a hero. I ran to the building without thinking, trying to save as many people as I could but on bringing out the 10th person the factory collapsed, so many lives were lost that day. Even though the war did not end but continued for a long time. Many men were compulsorily drafted and for someone like me who was regarded as a hero a greater burden was placed not only was I drafted into the army, I was also made to join the Alpha Team.

The Alpha team was a high intelligence war team that we had been hearing about for many years in Indiago. However, many thought it was a myth because no one had ever seen them. I was terrified, I was an ordinary factory worker two weeks ago, now they wanted to make me a member of the Alpha team? It would be better to prepare my mind for possible death. My opinion on the matter was not sought and I had to face war knowing I was on the most dangerous team and there was a possibility I would leave my little brother in this life.

The day I was to resume at the team base, Bert-my little brother-ran to me to give me a goodbye hug as if he could perceive the danger I was going into. His little body was shaking as he silently cried.

"Bert, why are you crying? I told you I would be back soon. Just in a few months, I will hug you again"

"But that's what Mom and Dad said and they never came back"

"Bert, look at me" I pulled back from him and stared into his baby blue eyes "I promise you I will be back" Those eyes lost some of their gloominess and he was able to manage a small smile. I ruffled his blonde hair and said "Be good for Mrs. Bingham, she will take care of you, ok?"

"Ok, take this", he held out the tiny cross necklace he had worn since childhood, it was his most prized possession " Give it back to me when you come home" I held on to him tightly again, inhaling his childlike scent, I had just made a promise I could not keep but I will do my best to come back alive no matter how hard it gets. I let go of it and walked to the truck waiting to take me to the Alpha Team bunker. I waved at my brother as I went on a journey I knew nothing about hoping that those who chose me knew what they were doing.

The truck drove endless for hours and I dozed off, at some point, it jerked to a stop and my eyes popped open.

"Are we there now?" I asked

"Yep," The driver, a huge man with a perpetually straight face replied. I had tried to start a conversation multiple times with him but eventually gave up. I looked outside the car, I didn't see any building in sight. It was just an empty grass field "Are you sure we are there?"

The driver didn't bother replying but clicked on a remote in his hands. A square portion of the grassland opened up and he drove our car in. This experience was looking unreal as it continued, I pinched myself to be sure I was not dreaming. Apparently, I was wide awake. The car entered some sort of underground high tech bunker. Everywhere was well lit and it looked as if I was transported to another world entirely. The door flung open and I was faced with a slim smiling man. His face looked somewhat familiar but I could not place it.

"Hi, Reinhard, it's nice to finally meet you" He knew my name

"Uh, nice to meet you too"

"Come on out of the car, let me brief you about the Alpha team"

I stepped out watching his animated face and trying to figure out who he was.

"So this is the Alpha team bunker, I'm sure you have heard a thing or two about us but many of it may be untrue while some may be true. First, we are not superhuman, we are normal human beings like you who have been specially trained for battle. We are only sent out for special missions. These missions are usually high risk and may determine the survival of our nation. 5 years ago the last Alpha team was disbanded and no one imagined that it would ever be created again but dangerous times call for dangerous measures. A few months ago I was contacted to be the captain of this team" He was walking backward while speaking to me and ran into someone that looked exactly like him with the exception of his smile. My eyes darted between the two.

"Meet my twin Andrew, we are co-captains of the alpha team. I'm Stephen". My eyes widened, I finally remembered why their faces were familiar. They are the legendary twins who won the international martial arts championship.

"You guys are the international champions. Wow, it's an honour to meet you! I follow martial arts and you are bosses"

"Nice to meet you too" They chorused

"Let's introduce you to the rest of the crew before we continue your briefing" I followed them to a well-lit room that looked like a cross between a gym room, a tech room, and a gun shooting range. A corner of the room was filled with computers and a young looking guy was typing endlessly on the computers. The gym section had different kinds of equipment and a huge man with brown hair and a lot of tattoos worked out. The shooting range had the tiniest member of the team shooting. Andrew whistled and everyone came to a standstill

"This is the newest member of our team, Reinhard. Reinhard, the guy staring at the computer is Fred, this huge guy is Pete and that lady is Nadine"

"Nice to meet you guys"

"Yes, nice to meet you" they echoed

Stephen held on to my arm and dragged me to another room, he made me sit while he and Andrew stared at me.

"What? Is something on my face"

"No..." Stephen said

"We are trying to figure out how you'll take this part of the briefing. So you must be wondering why you are here. You are not an outstanding fighter like Nadine and Pete and you are not into tech like Fred."

I nodded, wondering what they needed me for. I seemed like the weakest member in the group.

"First, know that what we are about to tell you is Alpha Team secret. No one outside here should know about it and they should not."

"Alright"

"Your mom and dad were originally citizens of Zavaka."

"You mean the country attacking us for no reason?"

"Yes. Zavaka originally operated the monarchical system until this current ruler usurped power. He had all members of the royal family killed and your mom was next in line to the throne so she was a target. That was when she fled Zavaka for our country Indiago."

My brain was taking time to catch up with this information. My mom was royalty! This was shocking.

"You look shocked, prepare for more shock," Stephen said while Andrew glared at him

"On arriving here they became the first members of the Alpha team. They were co-captains of the team"

"My mom and dad were part of the Alpha team? You want me to believe this? This is so farfetch'd"

"I have nothing to gain from lying to you. Did you never wonder why they went on extended vacations without taking you and your brother? Why were they so obsessed with your safety? Or why did they have few friends?"

All that he said was true but how could I believe that my mom and dad were not who I knew them to be.

"This is hard to process"

"I understand, they died on their last mission which is connected to the true cause of this war. While they were on their last mission, they had to cross the border to Indiago. It was at Zavaka they were captured and tortured till death"

I closed my eyes, holding back the years. I had always been comforted with the idea that my parents died in a car crash and that it was as fast and painless as possible. Now I know that they suffered torture for a long time before dying.

"The new ruler, Zyand, had a plan of capturing the world. As you know Zavaka has the most developed technology in the world. He was seeking to build a machine that would ensure world domination. This machine can cause devastation to a whole country at the press of a button. He has already been able to ensure the influence of this machine on neighbouring countries such as ours but he wants the whole world. In order to do that he needed a lot of funds that he does not have. He knew that the previous rulers had a safe where he believed so much gold was stored which would be enough to achieve his mission but he did not have the key. This was why he tortured your parents till death. He wanted the key but could not get it."

"So you're telling me that this Zyand can press a button and destroy our country right now?"

"Yes"

"Why doesn't he just do that instead of just bombing small parts of Indiago randomly?"

"He believes the key is still here and his plan is to capture Indiago, get the key, and then take over the whole world"

"Wow. I still don't get why I am here though"

"Just know that you are an integral member of the team and our mission may not succeed without you"

"What mission?"

Andrew looked at Stephen. This mission was definitely going to be a difficult one

"We are to kill the leader of Zavaka in order to ensure the safety of our nation"

I laughed for a few seconds till I saw their faces were serious

"You are joking, right? This is impossible. How exactly do you want us to penetrate Zavaka? Enter where Zyand lives in and kill him while he is surrounded and defended by millions of his army"

"The alpha team was created for practically impossible missions"

"I don't think I can do this"

"I think you should. Without you, onboard this mission may fail, and remember Zyand killed your parents"

I didn't know what to do, I was confused, going on the mission may mean that I would never see my brother again, yet it may be the only way to save my country.

"Please give me a few minutes to decide"

"Take all the time you need" Stephen and Andrew left me in the room.

For the first time in a long time, I missed my mother. I missed the way she would hold on to her cross pendant and mutter words of prayer. I missed her wisdom.

"What do I do?" I said rubbing the same cross pendant. It was at that moment I knew I was going to go on the mission even if it cost me my life. I wanted to rediscover the place of my parents' birth and meet the man who had them killed. I would do what my parents would have done and fight for Indiago.

The next few days were full of intense training. At the end of each day, my body ached and I slept deeply. I had a crash course on martial arts and shooting but I sincerely hoped I would not have to fight anyone because I didn't think this training was enough. At the end of seven days, the twins gathered us together and briefed us.

"Headquarters have sent instructions. It is time for us to go to Zavaka. Remember, that succeeding in our mission could save thousands of lives and failing could mean the end for Indiago"

That morning we packed our meagre load in our backpacks waiting for it to be night before we started on a journey that would determine the future of our nation. By night we were all anxious, no one could keep up the conversation, not even Stephen. We were anticipating the dangers to be faced on this journey and everyone faced some measure of fear. We snuck to the border of the two nations. They were separated by the small River Hari. We already got into canoes, as those were the most silent form of transportation on the river. By the time we crossed to the other side we all exhaled thinking the most difficult part was over. Suddenly, we heard dogs barking in the distance.

"Everyone lie down now!" Andrew said "Don't move at all"

The dogs drew closer and I held my breath, I was the one on the edge so if they would bite anyone first, it would be me. I laid down stiffly as one of the dogs began to sniff me. It was the longest minute of my life, I could not move because it could bite me so I had to wait for it to sniff and move away. Within a few minutes, the dogs dispersed. We stayed on the floor for a few minutes to ensure they were gone. After which, we all let out a sigh of relief.

"I never want to do that again," I said as I dusted off my clothes, Stephen and the others laughed but Andrew still maintained a straight face.

"We need to leave this place now"

We travelled on foot for the rest of the night. No amount of training could prepare me for the exhaustion I faced. By the time the sun was peeking out we had reached a city. Andrew quickly booked our accommodations and we soon had rooms to ourselves. I had to share with Fred but the guy didn't speak much so I didn't mind. Within a few minutes, I drifted off to sleep. The next time I would open my eyes it was already dark. Andrew had briefed us on our identity in Zavaka. I was a bartender while others had other roles.

We spent nights taking in Information and trying to strategize our mission. In a few days, we had gathered information about where Zyand lives and how to get there. However, Andrew was not satisfied with this bit and expected more information that may be useful on our journey. So we are out tonight again. The Capital city of Zavaka was always beaming to life after dark. It was not fake news that Zavaka was the most technologically advanced country in the world. They had robots attending to clients in the marketplace, dresses that change colours as instructed, various kinds of chips that could be inserted in a person's bloodstream to download information on any topic. Their tech scared me and made our impossible mission seem more impossible. Back to the night, we were all attending the Bachus club and made our way slowly into the glass building. We were going to spend the rest of our nights there. We mixed into the crowd when we got there. I sat on a barstool and acted friendly with the lady beside me trying to butter her up for information.

"Nice place, huh?"

She nodded her head noncommittally and continued playing idly with her drink.

"Have you been in this city all your life?"

"Yeah"

"I just moved to the capital a few days ago. Still trying to adjust to life here. I came looking for good fortune. I heard" I lowered my voice intentionally "the ruler lived in the capital and if you work as his soldier he pays very well"

"Huh huh"

"I'm trying to find where he lives. I want to apply to join his army"

At this, the lady's eyes suddenly had a spark. She gave a smile and held on to my arm, dragging me away from the club to the back alley of the club. I went with the flow thinking she looked harmless. I was very wrong. On getting outside before I could take a deep breath she knocked me out. The next time I opened my eyes I was tied to a chair but the funny thing was that I was not alone. All members of our team were tied to their own chairs. How did this happen? We were already busted before officially starting our mission. I looked at Andrew whose eyes looked like they were calculating some unknown formula.

"Hey, Andrew, do you have any idea how they got every one of us here?"

He shook his head and we went back to maintaining silence. After a long period had passed, the iron door to the place we were kept started squeaking. At last, we were going to meet our host.

"Guys, let me do the talking. Maybe we can talk our way out of here" Andrew said

About five people stepped in dressed in totally black clothes and standing in military formation. A woman stepped in after them and what I saw shocked me. She looked exactly like my mother, only younger. She walked up to my front and grabbed my chin and with a playful smile said

"Hello cousin"

"Cousin? I thought all members of the royal family were killed" I said glancing at Andrew

"My mother hid me in a secret passage in our house so even though they killed my parents in one day I was able to escape."

"Wow, so cousin huh? How did you know I was your cousin?"

"Oh I've done my research, and you do look a lot like your father. I've seen pictures and that was the only explanation I could have"

"Well you're right we are cousins but this" I held up my tied hands "was not the welcome I was expecting"

"The ropes must be quite uncomfortable but I want them in place while we discuss, once we arrive at an agreement you will be untied."

"I Immmmm and what are we discussing?"

43

"First, why are you here? I heard your mother fled to Indiago so you probably came from there. What are you doing in Zavaka?"

I glanced at Andrew, am I supposed to share the secrets of our mission with this stranger who was also family? He nodded, giving me a go-ahead. If we did not have them convinced we may die before we even start the mission anyway.

"Well, we are on a mission to assassinate the ruler of Zavaka in order to end this unnecessary war we are being faced with. Recently, Zyand has been bombing Indiago without being provoked so many people are suffering and I am sure you are aware that both the army and the weapons of Zavaka are too great for Indiago. Therefore, the only way we could possibly come out of this war is by removing the leader instigating the war."

She suddenly laughed loudly and motioned to her colleagues to loosen us

"I knew I liked you immediately when I saw you. It was quite unlikely that we would be on the same side but we are"

"What do you mean?" I stood up and stretched my body, the ropes had been tied so tightly that they had cut off blood flow to some parts of my body.

"Zavaka does not love Zyand but only suffers under his oppressive rule. After he forcefully took power many years ago Zyand killed a lot of people, not only the royal family. He was paranoid so anyone he felt was a threat to his power he had killed. He taxed the people heavily and people barely made ends meet. This is especially worse for those who are farmers, after harvesting so much food by the time Zyand's taxes are removed they barely have enough to live on. The suffering was so much but no one dared fight against Zyand, they feared for their lives.`` She cleared her throat "A few years back I started an underground revolutionary movement resisting the tyranny of Zyand. All those who supported the old monarchical system supported me but we have been faced with how to overthrow Zyand"

I looked at the tiny lady before me. She was leading a revolution? It was hard to believe.

"Are you looking down on me?"

"No no," I said quickly

"Anyway, if you can achieve your mission of killing Zyand we can succeed in our revolution. You do have a plan right?"

"We are still gathering information," Andrew said

"My people have been following you for 4 days. You still don't have enough information yet?"

We looked down, honestly, we had not figured out how we would break into Zyand's residence.

"Looks like I would have to help you do the mental work of your plan. I am Vicky by the way"

Vicky had created a massive underground movement. Thousands of people followed her and she had many trained soldiers. After giving them a place to rest that night, she met with them the next day.

"So let's get to work"

She clicked a button on her watch and a map that looked almost as real as paper hovered in the air.

"This map describes Zyand's residence. He lives in a castle that is heavily guarded and there are different lines of defence before you can get to him"

"Ok," Andrew said as we studied the map, the castle looked impenetrable and I was wondering why we had to follow through with a mission that was practically impossible.

"As you can see it is almost impossible to make it inside the castle but we are going to find a way. You are going to become a member of Zyand's army"

"What do you mean?"

"Zyand's army are those defending his residence and the only people allowed anywhere near him. We have heard rumours that Zyand is not a fighter, he is just a fat man standing behind his great army. So his army protected him heavily. One part of Zyand's army that you cannot fake is the tattoo on their left arm. They all have the letter Z in a circle tattooed into their arm. Also, you would have to dress like them and your face looks too Indiagonian. You would need a face moulding mask."

Vicky's men helped us with the tattoos and soon we were all spotting a Z tattoo in our right arm

"Are you sure this can be cleared?" Nadine asked with a frown. Going back to Indiago with the enemy's mark was not an option.

"Sure it can." The tattooist replied

Vicky also got us what she called face moulding masks. Before then I had never seen anything like it. It could be placed on a person's face and it would totally change the facial structure while looking very natural. She briefed us more about Zyand's castle. Pointing at a particular spot in the map she said

"Here is the simulation room. This is the last place you encounter before you enter Zyand's chambers. It is his greatest form of defence. All his soldiers are well trained in simulations and so could easily pass through but for those who have never experienced it, it could make them mad." I widened my eyes, it could make people mad "it's because it makes your worst nightmare feel like your reality and the only way to get through is to never forget at any point that it is not real. After getting through the simulation room you would be at Zyand's chambers but he hides behind an invisible wall that only he can disable. You have to find a way to make him disable the wall himself and step close to you."

"How do we do that?" I asked

"You have something he wants desperately so it should be easy"

"What is that?"

"The key to the Zavaka's treasure," She said pointing at the necklace Bert gave me.

"This is the key?"

"Yes. He has looked for it for many years so he would know if it is authentic or not and this is the true key"

The next day we were dressed in Zavakan clothing and on our way to Zyand's castle. We passed through the gates of the castle with no problem after showing them our tattoos. Once we were inside Fred went to work on his computer and hacked the central security system of the castle. We effortlessly entered various doors until we got to the simulation room.

I took a deep breath and stepped into the room with the others. Andrew and Stephen looked at each other before stepping in. Once in the room, I no longer saw the other team members of the Alpha team. I was back at home in Indiago holding onto the bracelet Bert gave me. I stood in front of Mrs. Bingham's house with the gift I had bought for him. On ringing the doorbell, Mrs. Bingham opened the door with tear stained eyes

"What is wrong?" I kept asking but received no replies. The first thing I saw in the house was blood, lots of it stained the floor. My mind could not process what I was seeing until I saw Bert lying in a pull of blood, his once blonde hair now bloody red.

I screamed, holding on to my head, this can't be happening, I can't live without Bert. My brother, my brother, no, no, no. In my panic, my hand touched my necklace and I suddenly remembered it was not real. It was just a simulation. I looked up and my eyes cleared, I could see the members of the Alpha team again and all their eyes carried haunted looks. No one bothered talking, we stepped out of the simulation room ready to finish our mission.

The first thing I noticed in Zyand's chambers was the way it was decorated in gold. Everywhere light touched sparkled. The man himself sat behind a huge desk with his hands hovering over a red button. What kind of destruction would that red button cause?

"Who are you people and what do you want?"

I went down on one knee like Vicky taught me and said "I have brought you great news sir. I have found the key to Zavaka's treasure" I held up the necklace, showing him the cross pendant. Like Vicky predicted, his greed caused him to remove the invisible wall and run out from behind his desk to look at the key. Quickly the other members of the Alpha team had him surrounded with a gun to his head. He was a fat man and his jaw dropped down while he wondered what kind of conspiracy could have caused his soldiers to turn against him. Almost immediately we heard banging at the door. He held a satisfied smile.

"My soldiers have been programmed to be aware when I am in danger and they would do anything to bring me out of here."

Fred worked his magic and the door to Zyand's chambers was locked, an iron barricade even came up from under it. It was at that moment that Zyand knew he had no hope of escape. He hit Nadine who was holding the gun to his head and slit his throat with a knife in an attempt to kill himself. The tyrant of Zavaka died that day and all the soldiers who had been programmed to serve him were finally free. Vicky became the ruler of Zavaka and called off the war against Indiago. She wanted me to stay on as one of her advisors but I was not willing to leave my brother alone in Indiago.

The Alpha team went back to Indiago in a Zavakan plane, with a treaty between the new ruler of Zavaka and the leaders of Indiago. We were treated as heroes and I was asked to stay on as a team member. I immediately rejected the offer, I wanted to be there for my brother, he did not need to lose another family member.

I got him a gift and stood in front of Mrs. Bingham's house. It felt like a deja vu of the simulation in Zyand's castle. On ringing the doorbell Bert opened the door and ran to hug me.

"You came back! Thank you for coming back" I was heartbroken for my brother who knew the pain of losing people he loved at such a young age but at least he had me.

"Sure buddy, I told you I would, didn't I? Let me let you in on a secret" I whispered in his ears "I am even a hero now"

"Like Batman?"

I chuckled "Better than Batman"

TANEZCOR PICTURES LLC & INTERNATIONAL INVESTORS
PRESENT

OMAR ZAHID'S

SWITCHER
STRIKES

FIXMAN VERSUS SINISTER

PROLOGUE

"Will," his mother called exasperatedly. "Would you just stop running around for once and just stay with the group?"

Little Will, who had run off a few metres away from his mother to practise the sword-fighting drill he had been running in his head all day, turned to stare at his mother. He saw the look of disapproval in her face, and rather than sulk back to her side. He giggled and started laughing. "I told you," his father said, "leave the poor boy alone. All he wants is to have fun. You're taking it away from him." "He can have all the fun he wants at home or in a closeted space," his mother replied. "We're on the streets, darling. Anything can happen." "Like what?" his father questioned. "Look around you, honey. There are people walking all around. Nothing spells safety better. Besides, he's only a few feet in front. We can grab him if we need to."

Will's mother, Martha, shook her head and huffed. Why did she even care? Henry would support his son with every breath he took. It was not enough that Will was their only child, he had to come into the world with alluring blue eyes like his grandfather, whom Henry also loved to a fault. Sometimes, Martha was glad that the old man had passed. He was the most manipulative human she ever knew.

Suddenly, there was an uproar across the road. Martha turned and saw a large group of Afro Americans spill out of a salon, yelling at each other. It was mayhem over there. Their altercation pervaded the perfect afternoon like a crack on a piece of fine china. "Get your fucking hands off me!" one of the guys yelled, pushing a scrawny looking guy off him. The guy staggered backwards and fell butt-first on the ground. "I'll beat your ass if you talk shit to me again."

Martha's eyes went to her son immediately. "Will, baby," she called, "come over here, quickly." She wiggled her fingers, beckoning for her son. "Oh, God," Henry complained, "why can't these guys keep their dirty laundry in. Do they always have to wash it out in public view?" "Will, now!" Martha yelled. Will seemed to have found more interest in the violence unravelling across the street. The scrawny black kid went after the guy who had pushed him, swinging a blow at him. His fist bounced off the guy's cheek, like a napkin wiping dust away from a surface. The guy flexed his jaw and brought the kid down with one huge blow. People on the streets gasped in utter horror. "Stay down, you stupid…" The guy did not finish the silence as a gunshot rang out, sending the entire street into pandemonium. "Shit," Henry said. Martha's eyes immediately flew to her son, who flinched as another gunshot rang out. She dropped the bag she was holding and ran after him. Gunshots began to come from every angle now as the group scattered. Henry ducked as he waited for his wife to get his son. Then the true horror unfolded in front of him. In an instant, Martha crumbled to the ground, screaming her lungs out. She lay on the ground, unable to move as blood spurted out from a hole along her spine. "Martha!" Henry yelled, running after her.

Little Will stood on the ground, bawling in tears as he watched his mother's face contort in pain. Then her face went dead still as a bullet hit the ground next to her and ricocheted into her head. Will jerked. He had never seen someone go from pain to quietness that quickly.

Larry Fixman

Larry Fixman rolled into Beach Town with his convertible. He had driven past the signboard a couple of minutes back and thought that it looked quite pedestrian. He had done light reading on the town before the trip and found out that the town was a tourist hotspot, especially during the summer. It was aptly named Beach Town because of the number of beaches it had. Larry was not exactly surprised by the choice of nomenclature. He could not see what else a town with more than ten beaches could be called. However, he thought that a town with such a reputation would have had enough annual income to fix up their signboard, and make it look more appealing. The signboard at the entrance looked like an inheritance, a relic of time that would have been at the museum if it were not so useless. At one time, the signboard would have been bright blue, with the fonts on it white and bold. Now, the weather had sucked off all the brightness from the blue, leaving behind a pale coating that was falling off the signboard in chips and patches. Rust had also intruded onto the structure, eating up most of the words, sparing only the B,E,A,H, and T,O,W,N in 'WELCOME TO BEACH TOWN.' However, whatever impressions Larry got from the signboard as he drove in, he lost it when he got to the town proper – well, most of it.

The streets were clean and almost glossy. It looked as though they had been recoated by tar recently. Although the building structure in Beach Town was mostly low-rise, they looked impeccable, like they had followed an accurate urban development building plan. It was more organisation that Larry had seen in most of the big cities he had been to. He was impressed. They even seemed to have an active tree plantation system. Unlike most towns undergoing civilization, Beach Town had not gone through a deforestation craze to create space for projects. There were a few trees after every two or three blocks. It was exciting. However, beyond the sturdy buildings, clean streets, and trees, Larry noticed something disturbing. There was an eerie silence over the town, an invisible cloud of gloom that was so thick, he felt he could touch it if he reached out hard enough. Everyone seemed to walk heavily, as though they carried a burden on their shoulders. Larry understood that a tourist destination like this would probably have gotten used to the presence of newbies at this point in their history. However, it was not enough explanation for why no one even bothered to look his way. The few who did, carried exhausted looks in their eyes. They were tired, immensely tired. It was pretty obvious at this point: something was wrong with the town. It was the reason he had come all the way from Chicago. But he did not expect to see proof this quickly, and so openly. The town did not even hide it. In Larry's experience, cities were great at hiding ills. They were so large and chimed with activity at every second, that if one blinked, they would have missed a lot. Tourist towns were like that in a way. They were like celebrity locations, full of glamour and glitz. That alone should be enough to keep some things under the carpet. But it was just as bad as he had heard if he could feel it in the air like a bad smell. As if on cue, a red van rushed out of the intersection on the left, nearly pitching into Larry. The street was filled with the sound of screeching tires as both Larry's convertible and the van came to a stop. Larry stared incredulously at the van's tinted windscreen as smoke rolled off its tires. He immediately looked at the traffic light ahead of the van. It was red. His was green. What the hell's going on here? Larry thought. No sooner had he had the thought, than the van's door rolled open and three tough-looking dudes strode towards him with their hands in their pockets. Larry knew what that meant. He dug out his badge from his breast pocket and reached into the glove box for his Glock 19 MOS 9mm handgun. Then he thrust his arm out into the air, holding out his badge. "If you fellas know what's good for you," Larry yelled, "you'd stop right there. If you have eyes, you'd know that I'm licensed to use deadly force, and I'll use it if you take another step forward." The guys stopped immediately and exchanged glances with themselves. "Shit," Larry heard one of them say. "He's a fed. Let's get out of here. He's a fed." All three of them turned back, got into the van and zoomed off.

Larry breathed a sigh of relief. The last thing he wanted was to be welcomed into this tourist town with gunshots and blood on the streets. Besides, it could have easily been his blood on the streets. Those guys did not look like the kind of people that would shy away from killing a federal agent. They just needed to act on instruction, that's all. Larry placed his Glock on his lap and turned the ignition. He caught a few people staring at him from the curb. He noticed, oddly, that none of them looked interested. Scared, yes. But they looked like violent exchanges like this were regular. Larry turned his eyes back to the road and continued driving through town. His next stop, the original stop, was the police station. He had a scheduled meeting with the Sheriff. His primary assignment had been to come here and hop on a case that seemed to be too heavy for the local police to bear. He had just been given an introduction a few seconds ago. He hoped that things did not get any hotter than that in the days to come.

Will Sinister

Will Sinister leaned into his plush leather swivel chair and stuck a freshly lit Cuban cigar in his mouth. He had just spent thousands of dollars to have the pack delivered straight to his office. He could not afford to have it delivered to his home. The last thing he wanted was having his mother shriek in his ears about how he kept dangerous company. His old woman had lost it a couple of years back and had gone coo-coo. But Will just could not bring himself to do the deed and send her over to a retirement home. Among many things, Will counted his mother as his burden. After her tragic accident, back when he was a kid, had gotten her paralysed from the waist down, Will had taken it upon himself to take care of her. His father had died in that accident, and he had blamed himself ever since. Sometimes, he thought that if he had just listened to his mother and stuck with the group like she had said, none of what had transpired afterwards would have happened. His father would still be alive to see him in a seat of power, and his mother would have been less of a screaming, bumbling idiot. He inhaled deeply and sucked on the cigar. Then he pulled it out of his lips and exhaled, bringing out the cloud of smoke in his lungs. He watched the smoke hang in the air for a while, crawling up ever so slowly and chuckled. You see that, Will, he thought. That's the sign of success. Of control and power. He bowled his hand into fists and tilted his face upwards as he spun around in the chair.

Suddenly, his telephone rang. He reached out for it. It was his secretary, Maya. "Sir, you have some visitors," she said. Will could detect traces of anxiety in her voice. And instantly, he knew who his visitors were. That's quite surprising, he thought. It's not that time of the month yet. He sighed. "Be a darling and send them up, Maya," he said.

In a couple of seconds, the door swung in and a trio of heavily tattooed men walked in. They were almost of the same height, 5 foot 9. But the man in front was bald and older than the two who flanked him. Will got up with a smile on his face. "Mario, my man," he said, coming up from behind the table. He towered a good five inches above the men in the room. But the lethal look on their faces were enough testament that Will's height did not match their power. Will shook hands with Mario, the bald guy in front, who was also clearly the leader of the group. Will picked up the pack of Cuban cigars from the table and offered one to Mario. Mario lifted his brows, impressed. He picked the cigar and nodded in gratitude. Then he had one of the guys behind light it for him. He settled into the chair in front of Will's table, and Will returned to his chair. "What brings you to my office today?" Will asked. "I wasn't expecting your visit until next week." "Yes," Mario said, puffing out smoke through his nostrils. "Something came up." Will leaned into his chair as his expression switched instantly. Now, he was all business. "What's that?" "Some of the boys said they ran into a problem earlier today," Mario replied. Will laughed. "Come on, Mario. This is my town. You guys are here under my protection. And you're the Mafia, what possibly could have been a problem for you guys?" "A federal agent," Mario replied coldly. The mirth vanished from Will's face. He leaned forward and placed his arms on the desk. "What did you say?" Mario sighed. "They ran into a federal agent, Will. What's that all about?" "Woah," Will raised his hands. "I wasn't aware a federal agent was coming here." "You're the Mayor. The town's yours, like you said, and you had no idea that a federal agent was on his way here?" "I'm not law enforcement, Mario. These things happen. But that's why we have eyes out there, isn't it? So that we don't get caught unawares." "The boss isn't happy about it," Mario said.

"He wants this resolved quickly." "You can tell the boss to chill." Mario flashed Will a furious stare at about the same time the muscles on the guys standing behind him twitched. Their reactions did not escape Will's eyes and he burst into laughter. "Come on, guys, chill. I didn't mean that the way you think it did. This guy is a federal agent. I can't just go out there and ask him to leave the town. That's not how these things work." Mario got to his feet. "Then we'll kill the woman then," he said. "The one who refused to cooperate? The sheriff? We'll kill her." "No, no, no," Will objected. "That's too rash. I've got an election to prepare for. I can't have the people thinking bad of me. You guys all know how important it is that I win at the polls. If I don't, you can all kiss goodbye to whatever operations you're running here. Because I assure you the other guys are not going to be as inclined to your vision as I am." "You won't have a post to go for, if this agent isn't taken care of." "Just relax," Will waved dismissively. "Let me play this my way. I'll keep a close eye on both the sheriff and the federal agent. If push comes to shove, we'll have to kill them." Mario gave Will an imperceptible nod. "I'll give the boss your regards," he said. "Please, do," Will nodded. The trio turned and walked out of the office. Immediately the doors closed behind him, Will reached for the phone and dialed Maya. "Come up here, now," he instructed. Will got to his feet as soon as Maya walked into the office. He covered the distance between them in two strides, and smacked her so hard across the face that she flew into the wall beside her. "Get up, you piece of shit," Will yelled, pulling Maya up by the scruff of her neck. She whimpered, burying her face in her arms. But that was the end to the tirade of physical assault today. Will strode back to his desk. "Will you tell me why I didn't know that a federal agent was coming into town!" "I tried to tell you, sir," Maya cried, "I tried to tell you yesterday, but you were out of town and said not to disturb you at all." "What about today?" "You told me the same thing." Will turned and looked out the window. His chest heaved as he tried to control his rage. Without looking at Maya, he told her to leave. The poor woman walked out of the office, carrying her cheek in her hands. It felt so heavy after the impact of the slap. She closed the door gently behind her and Will sat in his chair. So, the FBI has decided to stick their noses in stuff that doesn't concern them, huh? He thought. He chuckled and shook his head. He had worked so hard to get to his current position. He was not going to let anything, anything in the world, take it away. He had come from nothing, and he had sworn on his journey to power, that he would not stop until he had gorged himself full. This agent, he thought, he's nothing but a distraction, a stumbling block. From out of the blues, he got an idea. He picked up the telephone and rang Maya. She picked up on the second dial. "What's my schedule like tomorrow, Maya?" "Uhm," she sniffed, "You have an appointment with the local radio and TV station at the hours of 12 and 4 respectively." "Oh, great. Thank you very much, Maya," he smiled. "You're a darling." Will lolled back into his seat, grabbed one of the armrests with one hand, and held his cigar on the other. His eyes twinkled with delight as he hatched the next step in his plan. He was not going to let anyone bring him down. Never. After a couple of minutes, Will smashed the butt of the cigar on the ashtray. He slipped it back into the pack and got to his feet. He had to be somewhere at the moment. He readjusted his belt, ensuring that his shirt was properly tucked in. Then he grabbed his coat on the way out and shut the door behind him. "I'm heading out," he told Maya as he walked past her. "Keep me apprised of any important calls and messages that come in. I won't be coming to the office until tomorrow." "Yes, sir," Maya said. As soon as Will disappeared down the stairs, she looked at the ceiling and exhaled with relief. Then her eyes teared up, a prelude to a fresh sob. Will wrapped his coat around him as he walked towards his SUV. As soon as he got in, he placed a call to a discrete user. "Hello," Will said. "Is he awake?" "Yes," a gruff voice replied from the other end of the phone. "We've been keeping him busy." "Good. Remember the deal. Torture him, but don't inflict any lasting damages. I just need to shake that wanker, Flora Bills, a little so she can take a step back from contesting." "Yes, boss," the voice replied. "I'll check in later in the evening to see how things are going." "We'll be waiting for you." Will sighed as soon as the connection had ended. He stared at the rearview and powerful black eyes stared back at him. He was still in control, he reminded himself that. Some things had begun to slip through the cracks of his fingers of late, but it was normal. His father had told him when he was just a boy: "Absolute power, my boy, is never just absolute. There are times when you'd begin to lose your grasp. It's normal. Absolute power is when you continue to do everything to make sure that your grip is absolute. You get me?" Will had laughed at the lesson back then. He was not laughing now. He turned the ignition and zoomed off into the distance.

The Sheriff Laura Alens & Beach Town George

Larry sat on his desk, examining a dossier in front of him. It was one of numerous folders that had arrived at his home early this afternoon from the sheriff's office. However, he had phoned the sheriff, Laura Alen, a couple of hours ago, asking for a file on the mayor of the town, Will Sinister. At the moment, he was going through a folder that had listings of Mafia activity in Beach Town. Larry had gone through the files a couple of times, but there was something missing. The reports made it look like the Mafia presence had just materialised from nowhere. But Larry knew it was not true. Crime organisations like the Mafia were like viruses. They did not just come to a place fully formed. They started like a little stain, and when they found that the ground was fertile, they spread, eating up everything rapidly as time went by. Beach Town might have the most lovable sights in the country, but it had fallen prey to yet another mafia scheme. Larry suspected that their presence in the town was tied to Will Sinister. He had heard the stories before he came into Beach Town. Will Sinister was the man who ran things in Beach Town. No one so much as coughed without his permission, and you could lose your life by even staring at him the wrong way. However, there was no evidence on paper that Will had done any of these things. The allegations against him were pretty damning to have him arrested and tried in the courtroom, but that was impossible at the moment because of the immunity his political position granted him. Larry heard that it was election season and Will would be hitting the polls again. If he was successful, he would keep on perpetrating heinous crimes without any fear of arrest. Hell, without any fear at all. Larry smiled cynically. He's a smart one, he thought. Really smart. From where he sat, he heard a car pull up in front of his apartment. He picked up his Glock from the table and slipped it in behind his waistline. Then he walked towards the door and opened it. He felt at ease when he saw Laura step out of her truck. "Come to see if you were under attack, huh?" Laura joked. Larry smiled. "There's no harm in trying, is there?" "No, agent. None at all." Laura sized up the federal agent as she walked up the stairs to the porch. He was at least 6 feet tall, had a crop of brown hair, and a thick brown moustache. His eyes were twinkly, as though ideas were always sparking to life in his brain. He had an amused look on his face. "Laura Alens," she said, stretching her hand for a handshake. "We didn't have the pleasure of meeting when you stopped by the station." "No, we didn't," Larry replied, taking her hands. "I'm Larry Fixman by the way." "Welcome to Beach Town, Larry." "I seemed to have gotten an more proper welcome on my way to the station," he said as they walked inside. He told the sheriff about the incident with the guys in the van. "Congrats, Larry," she said, "you just met one of the thorns in Beach Town's backside, the Italian Mafia." "Yeah," Larry nodded. "I've gone through the files." Laura raised her brows as she bobbed her head. She was impressed. "Well, as for the file you asked for, we don't really have one?" "Why?" "Will's in charge here, Larry," Laura shrugged. "He's smart. He probably knows that people would want to use details of his life as a tool against him. So, he has any info about him redacted." "Are you saying no one knows a thing about him?" "Nope. People do," Laura replied. "They don't just know any of the deep stuff. And I'm sure that's what you're looking for." "Yeah," Larry nodded. "Well, if you've got spare time in your hands. I know of a place we can check. George." "George?" "Yeah. He's an old detective who came back to the town for retirement. He's one of the people who've been here for the longest. Those who can still remember the way things were before Will Sinister that is." "Alright. Let's go see this George then." George was sitting on his porch when the Sheriff's truck drove into his property. He did not take his eyes off it until it parked a few meters away from the front of his home. The sheriff stepped out and she was followed by a stranger. George narrowed his eyes. He had never seen the man in Beach Town before. He would have taken him for a tourist, but a tourist would not be taking rides in the Sheriff's car like it was a party bus. Laura smiled as she walked up to George. "Hello, George," she greeted. "I can see you're enjoying the evening air." George smiled. "I'm actually waiting for the sun to set. It usually goes down between those trees," he pointed into the distance. Larry turned, following the direction of the old man's finger and saw a couple of huge oaks in the distance. "Who's your boyfriend?" George asked. "Oh, please," Laura said, rolling her eyes. "He's not my boyfriend. George, this is federal agent, Larry Fixman. He's here to help us with out with, uhm, our rat problem." "Oh," George's eyes lit up. "News has gotten out then?" "Yes, it has, George," Larry replied. "But we can't do anything until there's been a due investigation." "Well, good luck with that," George said. "Your adversary is as ruthless as he is smart. You'll never actually catch his hands that dirty. Well, unless you know how to look." Larry smiled. "That's why I'm here." "Great. With that kind of optimism, you may be off to a great start. Or not." "I don't care about great starts," Larry said. "I only care about bringing a tyrant, if indeed Will is one, to his knees and making him suffer for all he has done. The sheriff said that you'd know somethings. So, I'm here to asks questions." George smiled. "By all means, come on in. What I'm about to say to you aren't the kind of things you speak about on one's porch." "So, what do you want to know?" George asked as soon as they settled down in his living room. "Anything you know about Will Sinister." George chuckled. "He has done enough to keep his name off most people's mouths." "But something tells me you're not one of these people," Larry retorted. "You're right. Well, if you intend to catch Will Sinister, you better do that before the elections. He's doing everything to make sure he curries favor again. This is the only window you'd have. At least until his tenure is over and it's election period again." Larry nodded. "Good. So, where do I start?" George asked. "From the beginning," Larry said. "Well, a couple of years back when I first returned to Beach Town, I did some digging on the guy. And here's what I found. The reason Will is such a hard stain to remove is that he grew up here in Beach Town. And though the whole town is scared of him now, he's still a darling. He's one of them. The only people who really see his ugly side are his opponents. You say one word against the guy, and you don't see daylight again. It's like you've vanished from the surface of the earth. Beach Town is like all towns regardless of how developed it is. They love their own, regardless of the stories they hear. You came here to liberate them, but you're the one they'd hate." "Wow," Larry said, lulling back into the couch. "That's quite a twisted relationship." "Hm," George shrugged. "The devil you know is better than the angel you don't." "True enough. What was his childhood like?" "He spent most of his time outside the town after his parents got into an accident." "What accident?" "Well, his parents got shot during a gang shootout…" "Here in Beach Town?" "Yes, of course. Gangs aren't foreign here, Mr. Fixman. If that was your perception. Get it out. It's only more prominent now because Will seemed to have given them free reign over everything." "Alright," Larry nodded. "Well," George continued, "his father died there at the spot while trying to help his wife who had already been gunned down. The wife survived, but she was paralyzed from the waist down and seemed to have little problem with her mental faculties. Well, no one knows where she is now. All I can say is Will left Beach Town and returned a changed man. He seems to have some vendetta for the Afroamerican demographic in town." "What do you mean?" Larry asked. "Well, there are oppressive polices regarding places they can go and all that. It's not that obvious? It's more like what you'd find in sundown towns. There are more cop presence in the Afroamerican sections, the bail system is almost nonexistent when an Afroamerican is arrested and so forth. Apart from that, everybody knows not to go head-to-head with Will. He is good-looking and is armed with the most gracious smile you'd ever see. But he's a devil." And I'm here to send him back to hell, Larry thought. I'm here to fix the town. On their way back to the truck, Laura spoke to Larry. "You know," she said, "I don't know how you intend to go about fixing this whole debacle. But just know that I'm with you on it." Larry nodded. "Thank you. But I'm not sure you had any other option." "Why? Because you think I'm obligated to help you as sheriff?" "No," Larry said. "You could just have easily told me to go eat shit from my first day here. You, on the other hand are here with me because you're not corrupt. If the mayor's got some cops on his side, you're not one of them. I don't know what shitshow he's been running here, but I'm about to get to the bottom of things." As Laura drove Larry home, he asked her if there were any weak links to Will. "No," she replied. "Nothing. Anyone who gets close enough to him, disappears." "Wow," Larry nodded. "This guy must be a magician." "Oh, he is. I'm shocked that he hasn't even come for me." "Oh, let him come. I wish he would." Laura looked at the federal agent. The gleam in his eyes was still there. She could not tell if he thought this was a game, but she liked the courage and fervor with which he spoke. He may not be successful at flushing out Will Sinister, but she liked him because he had the will to try.

* * *

In the following days, Larry and the sheriff worked quite closely. They did everything from going through files together to going out in the field to ask questions. Most of the people they met were cold and unwilling to be party to any form of interrogation. On the first day, alone, Larry knew that if he had not come out with the Sheriff, he would have gotten nada. They moved from asking the townsfolk questions about their mayor, to busting in on small Mafia operations. "It's not been done before," the Sheriff objected when Larry had suggested the move. "Nothing will stop them from getting violent.'" "You don't understand, Laura," Larry said. "All this is a game at this point. You have to look at it like chess. There are moves and countermoves. Will is a smart man and likes playing things close to his chest. But this is a chessboard and there is more than one way to force his hand." "I don't think that's a good idea, Larry. Everyone here knows what it's like when you force the mayor's hand." Larry laughed. "Will may not be afraid of anything. But you'd find out that pocketing a federal agent is more difficult than, say, having the entire local police force dancing on the tip of his fingers. I intend to use that to my advantage. Will won't go for me at first. He'll try to see if I can play ball. That's my chance to get closer to him. You can learn a lot about someone by just being a few feet away from them." Laura had marvelled at his conception. It was simple, but it was a masterstroke. So, she was not surprised when Larry told her that Will had invited him to his office for a short tete-a-tete. They had burst into three Mafia drug operations within that week. Like Larry had projected, it was bound to make Will react. Now, he had not only given himself access to Will Sinister, but it had also turned a suspicion to fact. Will Sinister was in league with the Italian Mafia. Larry rolled his convertible in front of the mayor's office. The mayor had suggested that they meet after dark. But Larry had insisted on an afternoon meeting. No matter how much power they exerted over the town, it was easier for the Mafia to make moves under dark than in broad daylight. Too much publicity was still bad news. It had already drawn the attention of one federal agent. It could draw more. Larry arranged his collar and walked into the office. He exchanged warm pleasantries with the receptionist who sent him all the way up to the mayor's office. The mayor's office was a two-room structure that occupied most of the second floor of the two story building. The first room was the waiting area and also served as the secretary's office. As soon as Larry walked in, the secretary, a young redhead, who Larry thought would be in her late twenties, pointed at one of the padded chairs in the room. "He's on a call and will be with you shortly," she said. Larry nodded and took a seat. He crossed his legs and took a cursory look around the room. However, nothing was of more importance than the secretary pretending to be busy on her computer. He had noticed her stealing glances at him when she thought he was not looking. Now that he was, she was busy clacking away at the keyboard. In his experience, people did not look at you that way if they were not interested. He studied her face – the red lipstick, thick brows, blue eyes, but most of all her makeup. He realised that there was an oddity with the way the makeup was applied on her face. There were patches on her face, spots where there had been more. And that was strange. Every other thing on her face was perfectly done; from the lipstick to the brows. It did not make sense that she would mess this up. There were slight, almost imperceptible patches, where she used a concealer. And concealers only had one use in a woman's makeup. To hide. The real question now was what she was trying to hide, and Larry was curious about that. The door to the mayor's office swung open and Will stepped out. "Hey, I'm so sorry to keep you waiting," he said. At that moment, Larry got his opening. He noticed the secretary flinch slightly as soon as she heard Will's voice. She crossed eyes briefly and looked away. I knew something was wrong, Larry thought. "Please, come in," Will said. Larry followed him inside the office. Will Sinister's office was more opulent than most public offices he had been to. The room was longer than he had expected, and was heralded by a lounging area consisting of four couches placed in a quadrant. They were wrapped in plush green velvet. There was a Persian rug right in the middle with a glass coffee table on top. His office desk was way in the back, a large mahogany table with expensive leather covering. The walls were a cross between burnished wooden panels and ornately designed wallpapers. There was a small chandelier hanging down from the office. It was as if the mayor had taken the term "feel at home" quite literally in his office. "Please, sit," Will said, pointing at one of the couches. Larry took it and Will sat opposite him. "What would you like?" Will asked. "I've got champagne, I've…" "Water will be fine," Larry said. "But refreshments aren't at the top of my mind right now." Will smiled. "I like you already. Straight to the point. That's my Modus Operandi as well." He leaned back into his chair and appraised the federal agent from the corner of his eyes. He did not yet know if this guy was the kind he could buy. So far, he was putting up a tough act, but Will knew that even tough people could get broken. "Anyways," Will started, "I'm Will Sinister, I'm the mayor of Beach Town, I'm the Beach Town, but you must know that already. Quite frankly, I'm happy that you're here. There have been dastardly acts in Beach Town by its criminal elements for a while now. And the local police have been quite inept when it comes to dealing with it. So, I appreciate the show of concern by those at the federal level. It's touching, really. However, what you might not know, Mr. Fixman, is that running a town is incredibly delicate work." Larry smiled. He had not even introduced himself, and the mayor already knew him by name. Will had already done his homework. "So delicate," Will continued, "that everything could break in one second. Beach Town might be a source of joy to the people who live here, but they're also aware of how fragile our peace is. I've received reports that your investigative efforts have been, uhm, how do I put this? They have been rattling a few nests. I'm not trying to tell you how to do your job. But I'd love it if you didn't make mine difficult." "God forbid that I do something like that," Larry said with a shrug. "I simply cracked down on Mafia operations in your town, Mr. Mayor. You should be thanking me." "And I am. Truly, I am. But things are fragile here. You've only been here like what? Three weeks? I've been here forty-something years." "And going for an extra term I hear," Larry quipped. Will laughed. "Yes. So, you do keep your ears to the ground." "Of course," Larry smiled. "How else do you expect to be aware of your surroundings?" Will nodded. Both men stared at each other, one sizing the other up in his mind. It was like a battle. "What I'm trying to say, Mr. Fixman, is that you may be the better investigator, but I have extensive experience with Beach Town. There are a lot of demographics here, and I'm solely in charge of making sure everyone co-exists peacefully. The tension can be quite unnerving sometimes. You're lucky you came in here when things are already quiet. Let me tell you something, a confession if you can see it that way. I'm sure you came here because of the kidnappings and killings that have been going on here. All these crimes are enough to close down the town and have all 50, 000 of its residents run off into hiding. But I've still got it up and running. I'm only asking that you don't destroy what I've set up. Already, people are already accusing you of being targeted." Larry chuckled. "Some people may say the same thing about you, Mayor." "Excuse me?" Will frowned. "I'm just saying, word flies around you. The afroamerican community can also accuse you of being targeted in your treatment towards them." Will stared at Larry for a second before speaking. "I advise strongly, while you're here, Mr. Fixman, to not base your investigation on hearsay. Perhaps, that's why you already have a quadrant of the town agitated." "No, Mr. Sinister," Larry replied firmly. "I've rattled the criminal underbelly of this town. I made arrests of members of the Mafia, and I've handed them over to the police for questioning. I came here for an investigation, and that's what I'm doing." Will heaved a sigh. He was getting impatient with Larry's daringly indifferent attitude. It was certain by this time that this was someone he could not control. But it did not mean that he could not silence him. "Listen, Mr. Fixman, if you won't, at least, listen to my suggestions, I may have to place a call to your superiors and have you removed. And if I have to do that, you won't have a job to go back to, believe me." A sly smile grew on Larry's face. He recognized a threat when he heard one, and the Mayor of Beach Town had just threatened him. Larry chuckled. "You can do that," he said. "I know you have tons of connections. But shouldn't you have asked yourself some questions? No one's been able to attack the Mafia before? If I'm doing it, it should instigate some questions. For instance, I might have, beyond ever reasonable doubt, evidence that validates my arrests, evidence that validates every single move I make." Will had a scowl on his face now. "I'm not stupid, mayor," Larry continued. "I'm here for something. I knew what I was coming into. And I came prepared. Now, the stakes are clear. I either get beat, or I win. It's that simple." Will smiled. "You know," he said, "I wouldn't have expected this level of dedication to a righteous cause from someone who left his best friend to die." The smile on Larry's face vanished as Will stared pointedly at him. "But again," Will continued, "I understand the guilt that must plague you, and the necessity to make up for it by trying to stick all your nose where it doesn't belong. But you should be careful. Don't let it push you into biting off more than you can chew." Will saw the hesitation on Larry's face and he suppressed a smile. The federal agent had thought he had had him by the hooks all this time. He was wrong. He could run background research almost as quickly as the detective could. "It was nice meeting you, mayor," Larry said, getting to his feet. "We may see each other again or not. But don't worry, I won't be the one disturbing the peace of your precious town. Say hello to your mother for me. I'll show myself out." Will glowered as Larry waltzed towards the door and shut it behind him. "*That peacock*", he thought. "*You and that stupid sheriff are about to learn the lesson of your lives.*" He picked up his phone and dialled a number immediately. "Yes," he said when the call went through. "It's about time." Larry hesitated by the secretary's desk when he walked out. Without warning, he grabbed a pen and paper from her desk, and scribbled his number on it. Then he placed it in front of her and walked away. Maya stared at the writing on the paper. It was the agent's phone number above the words: "Call me." She immediately crumpled it up and tossed it inside her drawer.

* * *

Larry got his call later that evening. He knew for a certainty that it was going to come, and it had been revealing. Will's secretary told him everything from how he had strange meetings with dangerous looking people, to how he beat her up, and how she had overheard him make threats to certain people. She mentioned Flora Bills, who was also running for the post of mayor in the upcoming elections. Larry advised her to stay low and report to him if there were any other changes. He relayed Maya's message to the sheriff when she dropped by at his home. He had turned his living room into an office, and he often spent most of his time there now. He had bought a board from the supermarket, and now it was filled with images and red connecting lines. At the centre of it all was Will Sinister. "Flora Bill's husband just went missing a couple of days ago," the sheriff said. "She's been making frequent calls to the police station asking for updates. But it's useless. Almost half of the force is in Will's pocket." "Of course, I don't expect anything less. But you have a suspect?" "Of course, Will Sinister. He knows that if he loses the polls, he loses his immunity. Flora has been racking up the people's interests.

She's also been in Beach Town since she was little, and Will's beginning to see her as a threat. The last time she called me, she was considering trying to step down. The stress of looking for her husband and campaigning at the same time was getting too much." Larry shook his head. Will was good, but he was also proud and pompous. If there was one thing he realised while speaking with him in his office, it was that he was power-drunk. The furnishing in his office, his mannerisms, everything said that he did not intend on relinquishing his power any time soon. And Larry knew one thing about power-drunk people. They didn't care for anything else besides brandishing their power. Will had it now, and he could accomplish a lot with it. He already knew that Larry was not going to back down. So, Larry expected him to do something to keep the investigation quiet. Already, by going for the Mafia, he had rattled, not just the criminal underworld itself, but the spate of dirty secrets that could be hung out in the open. All Larry had to do was get one of the criminals to talk. Larry was just about to go make coffee when a flood of bright lights hit him from the window. He squinted in confusion. Those look like headlights, he thought. And then it hit him with bone chilling certainty. Larry only had a moment. "Get down," he yelled, diving into Laura and bringing her to the ground. As soon as he hit the ground, a barrage of bullets tore through the window, shattering the glass to pieces and tearing up the wall above him. "Oh, my God," Laura exclaimed in shock. "They're here." "Yeah," Larry said. "You'd have to fight like the devil if you want to see another day. Such a bold attack means they're here to kill us." Larry covered his head with his arms as a fresh wave of bullets burst into the room. And then it stopped. "Larry Fixman!" Will's voice came from outside. "Laura Alen, please come out now, and I promise we can talk about this." Larry rushed to the corner and pulled out the bag he had stashed his ammo in. He did not have anything other than his Glock, but it would suffice. Will's biggest mistake would be to underestimate him. He pulled out his phone and began to record. Laura met his eyes and then Larry winked at her. She was astonished, not just with Larry's bravery to record while his life was in danger, but by the act itself.

He was getting evidence. "Come out now, guys," Will continued. "You don't have to die. I'm sure we can work something out." "The only thing we can work out right now," Larry yelled, "is your surrender." "Come on, now," Will called. "There's only two of you and five of us. Larry, I've read your file. You barely even passed shooting classes. They sent you here because it was either that or return to the desk. Please, don't do this to yourself. There's a place where we both benefit from this." "You've spoken to me already, Will Sinister," Larry yelled, "you already know what my answer is going to be." "Very well then," Will called back. "You brought this on yourself." Larry ended the recording and gave the phone to Laura. "Get out of here. Now," he instructed. "Get out through the back door at the kitchen." "Are you crazy?" Laura replied, bewildered. "They're going to…" "Do your job, sheriff. And just take this out. If this is safe with you, it'd be easier to pin down Will Sinister for his crimes. Now get out of here." Laura was still reluctant but Larry grabbed her by the shoulders and she obliged. As soon as she walked through the door to the kitchen, the front door came down. The first three people that walked in got a bullet straight to their heads. That's what happens when you underestimate someone, Larry thought. That was three down and two to go. Larry sensed that Will would likely be on the run if he saw him down three of his men in such a short time. He could not let him go back for reinforcements. Quickly, he got out from behind the couch and moved towards the door, crouching the entire time. It was advantageous that he was quick, because as soon as he stood beside the door, he saw the muzzle of a rifle move inside from outside. Larry waited, until he could see the intruder's arm. Then he shot a bullet in it, grabbed the arm and pulled the body of the screaming guy in front of his own. That quick thinking saved his life because Will started pumping bullets in Larry's direction, yelling with each shot. The bullets perforated the body of the guy Larry used as a human shield until his torso was a mix of tattered skin, bone, cloth and a lot of blood. Larry smiled when he heard Will's gun click. The chamber was empty. He let his human shield fall to the ground. "My turn," Larry said. He rushed towards Will, while he still struggled to load his gun and slammed the muzzle of his Glock into the side of his head. Will's gun clattered to the ground as he collapsed. Then he used his hands to pull himself away from Larry. "How?" he asked, confused, "but your file…" "Was a misdirection," Larry interrupted. "I'm an Army Ranger, made a switch to the FBI after my first tour in Afghanistan. I couldn't deal with the war, but I knew I wanted to help anyway I could within the country. So, I started doing this." Larry chuckled. "The thing about power, Will Sinister, is that it makes you drunk and blind. You're smart, but you have power. And power can be an instrument of control for the man that owns it and it can also be used to control the man that owns it. Anyone who understands that can wrap up cases like this in a blink. All I just had to do was confront your ego. Now, you're in for it." "You can't do anything to me," Will said. "I've got reinforcements coming. This is my town. You can run if you like, but you'd be dead before you cross the borders." Will had barely finished his words when Larry swung his gun into the side of his head, sending him straight to sleep. "Don't worry, man," Larry said, "I'll take my chances." He pulled Will's phone out of his pocket, took pictures of his unconscious face, and did the same thing with the bodies of the men he had brought with him. He would send the pictures of the men back to the headquarters so they could run a facial recognition scan. Will was done for. All Larry was doing now was gathering enough evidence to put him away for a very long time.

BY HOOK OR BY CROOK

The plains were cruel any other time of the day, but at the dead of night they sang ruggedly. Its song was not the kind gotten from any guitar, flute, or provoked sermoner in the wild west. It lay hidden, invisible in the howl of the dry wind, kicking up dust and dead twigs, and rustling out dangerous secrets from within the eye of shadows. There was a long list of dangerous things. A rattlesnake was dangerous, yet for all their bite, they lacked stealth, choosing to leave that to the jurisdiction of Indians with easy prey on sight. And a group of them were currently closing in on a lone sleeper, mad enough to light a fire in these parts.

The Indians, five of them, looked at each other. Their eyes gleamed with the glee of an easy kill. Their rough brown faces, covered by grotesque painting, made them look like monsters from the depths of hell. Their prey was an unknown figure in a dirty brown shirt, tucked into black trousers. The head rested on a small rise on the earth with a hat sitting over the entire face. His feet, clad with thick leather brown boots and semi-rusted spurs, rested close to the fire.

The Indians looked around. There was no horse, no other signs he was with company. He was truly an easy kill. They crouched forward, prepping their axes and knives for the death strike.

Suddenly, their prey spoke.

"Pardon me for asking, but you folks don't happen to know the way to the Golden City now, do you?"

His voice was croaky, like gravels rolling against one another in a tumbler. And coming from underneath his hat, it had an eerie quality.

The Indians stared at each other. Maybe, he wasn't exactly an easy kill, but he was still grossly outnumbered. Five to one was too bad an odd in the wild.

The Indians whispered something among themselves.

"Huh?" the man asked. "You folks would have to do better than that if you want to help a man."

The Indians began to speak hurriedly among themselves, and then a gunshot rang out, shattering their heated conference. They shuddered, then turned to themselves. That was when they saw it – the stream of blood spurting exuberantly from the neck of the youngest in the group. They turned back to the man in the boots. He held a pistol close to his side, and wisps of smoke coiled off its muzzle.

"I have no time for bastards," he said, "especially those who disturbed my rest."

One of the Indians yelled something in rage, lifted his axe high in the air, and charged. The man let fly a stream of bullets, moving his hand around blindly. For a while, the sound of gunshots echoed through the air like a song until the pistol's chamber clicked. He was out. But the ensuing silence was more forthwith.

He pulled the hat off his face and sat up, coming into the light. A lopsided grin sat on a face as harsh as the dry wind. A long scar ran across the entire length of his face. His nose was a little crooked, but his jaw was set and hard; his eyes, a sparkling blue under the fire.

He sighed and got to his feet.

"When will they ever learn?" He asked himself. "John's a long shot. Probably, the longest shot in the whole wild west."

He reloaded his pistol, and had just slipped it back into his holster when he heard a weak groan. John stared at the corpses of dead Indians in front of him, and saw one of them move. A glint of mischief crawled into his eyes.

He walked over to the sole survivor of his fanatical shootout. He was trying to crawl towards the axe lying beside him.

"Don't worry," John said. "Let me help you." He drove his boot into the man's neck, snapping it in half. He sighed with satisfaction. "There. I'll see you in hell."

John turned around. He couldn't be far from the Golden City. But he needed a horse.

"Where there's an Indian, there's always a horse," he said out loud. He picked up his hat and placed it firmly on his head. Then he stomped on the fire, plunging himself into the dark, and walked away.

Not too far away, he stumbled upon a group of five horses. He whistled and approached them.

"Golden City, here I come."

Golden City was a detached town renowned for the insane gold rush about two decades ago. People from outside trooped towards the little settlement, shattering its peace and organisation. Everything in it now was built around the rush that followed the sudden discovery of gold. It was far rarer to find gold of recent, but the town had grown enough to have a life of its own. Still, there was still that distrust against foreigners that hung over the people like a shadow. And it followed John as he walked into the town on horseback, towing four more horses behind him.

Every single soul turned to look when he walked past, their eyes glowing with hostility. But John kept his face steely underneath his hat. His eyes stared straight ahead. He may have just been walking in a different world of his own. He was here for one thing, and one thing only.

He stopped the horses in front of a bar and got off. He looked around, staring at the hostile faces of the townspeople. Then he chuckled and tapped his horse by the side.

"Don't go anywhere. All of you." He pointed at all five of them.

Then he climbed up the stairs, and used his body to push through the doors. As soon as he walked in , a sudden hush fell on the entire bar. All eyes were on him, and just as quickly, the wanted poster by the doorposts. John turned, and stared at the posters. A hand-sketched picture of him stared back, with his full name 'John Grisham' underneath. He was wanted for the robbery of ten trains and the murder of 87 people.

John whistled. "They can't even give a man his rightful numbers in these parts."

Well, after tonight, he thought, *those numbers would have gone up.*

He turned and faced the full glare of the whole room. Then he tapped his holster, smiled daringly, and moved towards the counter.

He stared at the attendant, a buxom woman with breasts swelling like bread above her dress' neckline. She approached him hesitantly as if he was a time bomb.

"Two whiskies, please", John said.

The bar-woman had two glasses in front of him in no time.

"Pardon me, uhm, missus," John said. "I need some help finding the Crow Brothers. I hear they've got a settlement here, and are right here in town at this very moment."

The bar-woman looked around.

"What business do you have with the Crow Brothers?"

"Business." John downed two of the glasses, and placed a dollar bill in front of her. "Now, if you'll point me the right way, I'll be out of here as quick as a buck."

"I'm sorry", the woman stepped backwards, "I don't know where they are."

John hesitated a little. Then he smiled. He withdrew the dollar bill, and placed a couple of pennies on the counter instead. Meanwhile, he'd spotted one of the men in the bar, at the table just behind him, get up and reach for his rifle.

With speed like lightning, John pulled out his pistol, pulled his right shoulder down, and blew off the man's fingers through the opening between his left arm and his body.

The entire bar erupted in shock as blood sprayed across the man's table, into his wine glasses and on a few of his friends. His cries were loud and bloodcurdling. John stared at the entire lot of shocked faces out of narrowed eyes. Then he got up, blew the smoke off the muzzle of his gun and slid it back in his holster. He caught movement to his right and turned. His brows arched immediately.

There was a quiet, stunningly beautiful lady sitting alone on a table. She drank alone too. John found it puzzling that none of the men there had thought to bother her. She looked at him, but only for a moment. But even then, John had noticed the flash of desire in her eyes. He smiled.

He didn't know much about the girl, but he didn't need to. There was no helping it if a pretty girl like that couldn't resist him.

He walked over to her table, and sat in the chair across from her.

The girl looked at him. Without taking her eyes away, she leaned back into her chair, and spread her thighs wide apart. John noticed the move with a flicker of his eyes, and he restrained a smile.

"So what does the famed, evil, John Grisham want in the Golden City?"

John noticed how she stared directly into his eyes, how her face showed no signs of fear, and how freakishly unblemished her skin was. The mascara around her eyes made them look like pools of light emanating from the depths of darkness. Her lips were full and bright red; the heave of her plump breasts, inviting.

John looked at her musingly. "I'm here to see the Crow Brothers", he replied.

"Just them? No one else?" She shrugged.

"I didn't come here for gold, I can tell you that much."

The woman bit her lips. There it was again – that flash of desire in her eyes.

John harrumphed. "Although", he continued, "there are other things more precious than gold. And I'd be a madman if I didn't appreciate them."

He gave a lopsided smile, and the woman returned one of hers.

John burst out the bar's backdoor being led by the hand. The woman turned and gave him a wink. John chuckled. She pulled and he followed until they got to a farmhouse a few minutes away from the bar.

"This is where you live?" John asked as they stopped in front of the door.

"Surprised?"

"Not at all. If a girl works hard, she ought to be able to live according to her means."

She opened the door, and beckoned John in. As soon as he walked in, he knew something wasn't right. He heard the door close behind him. He turned. The gorgeous lady was nowhere to be found. He turned around again, and a group of six men stood in front of him. It was as if they'd appeared out of thin air.

"Setup," John said under his breath. "Someone can't even get a good fuck in these parts anymore."

"Look," one of the men, their leader, said. " If it isn't John Grisham in the flesh."

John compressed his lips hard as a steely expression crept into his face. "It's the Crow Brothers, yeah?"

"What business do you have here?"

"I'm here to kill you."

The brothers looked at themselves. Then they burst into laughter. John bit at the inside of his cheek until he could taste blood.

"You've come all the way here," the leader continued, "to kill us. My man, you're dead then. The only thing you had on us was a few seconds of surprise and you threw that out the window."

"You killed my brother," John growled.

The leaders' brows arched. Then he looked at the rest of the group. He stuck his thumbs into his belt hook, and danced a little on his legs.

"Let's assume," he said, "that we care about such an inconsequential piece of detail, who, pray tell, is your brother?"

"Gary the Devil."

The man shook his head. "Doesn't ring a bell. Look, man, we're not in the mood to shed blood today, or you'd have been dead the very moment you walked through those doors. Don't think about the death of your brother. It's going to get you killed. It's fair game. You're a killer too. You're no different than us."

"Except we're better," one of the brothers chipped in.

Their leader laughed. "Forget about this," the leader continued. "Out in the wild, you either kill or get killed. Every death is fair game. Make peace with it or you'll end up just like your sharpshooter wannabe brother."

"I thought you said he didn't ring a bell!" John yelled.

The leader clucked his tongue. "I said that, didn't I? Well, I meant he is so inconsequential to be talked about. He's dead. We talk about living. Not the dead."

John's heart felt like a volcano long overdue for eruption. It was filled with pain, anger, and hate. And it burst out.

"You fucking bastard!" he yelled. He whipped out his gun and fired a shot through the leader's head, spattering his brains on the face of the man behind him.

However, the Crow Brothers were no slouches. They returned fire almost immediately, and a bullet caught John dead in the shoulder. He grunted as his face contorted in pain. Then he dove out of the way of a hail of bullets.

His shoulder buffeted his fall as he crashed into the wall. He grimaced in pain, and righted himself.

"Fucking cowboy life", he cussed.

One of the brothers came into his line of sight, and he fired a shot into the centre of his face. "That's for Gary."

John started to get to his feet when a bullet missed his head by a hair's breadth. He ducked and ran for cover. He pushed through a door and found himself in the kitchen. He checked the chamber. He only had two bullets left.

"Shit."

His eyes fell on a knife on the counter. He picked it up and waited behind the door. As if on cue, it swung open and one of the brothers walked in. Their eyes met at the same time, but John moved quicker.

He swiped hard at the man's fingers, slicing them off. His gun hit the ground along with a couple of severed fingers.

The man started to scream but John slammed the knife right into his mouth, shutting him up forever.

John heard the sound of footsteps approaching and he jumped back. One of the men rushed inside, and John shot him at the back of the head.

Suddenly, John heard a click. He turned and saw one of the brothers, the youngest of them, pointing his pistol at him. John grinned. The man was out otherwise, he'd have been dead.

"What do you say we settle this man-to—"

The man's lips burst into a spray of blood and flesh as a gunshot rang out. The man hit the floor with a violent thud, and John blew the smoke off the muzzle of his gun.

"I was already tired of this soiree anyway," he told the dead corpse.

He turned and headed for the door, the left side of his shirt completely soaked in blood. He winced as the bullet wound on his shoulder screamed, but he walked with a certain purpose. He'd sated that insatiable craving to kill the men that murdered his younger brother. Up until that moment, there was nothing more he wanted.

He stepped out of the house and inhaled the air outside.

"It's a cowboy's life for me," he said.

Then he limped into the night.

KALEIDOSCOPE

When I was a small child, I got a little kaleidoscope from my parents and I hid it under my pillow.

Since then I have been travelling the infinite mysterious worlds created by the small colourful crystals of the kaleidoscope.

I have painted fictional maps and travelled to distant places on my bed.

Later, in my life, when I acquired so called life experience, I have learnt to be aware that I am actually dreaming in my dreams when I sleep.

And I was basically practising lucid dreaming. So in my dream, when I was sleeping, I was aware that I'm in fact dreaming.

It didn't always work, but I did practise the thing and I still keep practising it.

What can it help you with?

It's basically..., we sleep one third of our life and we can use dreams for adventures, for learning insights, acquiring hints on what to do in real life and so on, whatever...

You can use lucid dreaming as a white board, where you can draw and test the things, what could work in real life and what not. And then apply it as you are "awake".

When I was practising lucid dreaming, as time went by, I got a little bit lost along the way in so-called "real life", and like the majority of people, I was hypnotised, like a pigeon, by the flags moves.

And I was chasing all those dreams, money and success, powered by my ego and basically it was the road to nowhere.

Eventually I got burnt out.

One night, when I fell asleep, I had a dream that I met my future-self, in a matter of fact - the best version of myself from the future or another dimension.

It appeared in the form of an angel. The angel introduced itself, but warned me never to mention its name. I never did.

The angel shook my hand and said that everything will be fine.

Then the entity disappeared.

Well, since then, the angel appears from time to time in my dreams and gives me advice.

Sometimes this entity also appears in real life…, it rather communicates with me through the signs on billboards or T-shirts, via the mural paintings.

When I sleep, the angel visits me, sometimes we speak and sometimes we keep silent.

The angel frequently underlines three main points, to keep in mind in so-called "real life".

First: "I'm the source."

Second: "We're one."

Third: "We live in a collective dream."

Since then, everything in my life is turning for the better, I have to say and I have to thank God and my personal angel - the best version of myself.

If I'm aware - in my "real life" - that I'm actually dreaming, I can control myself better and I can better influence how I communicate, how I interact.

And basically I can achieve any goal I dream about, any target I set.
And you could do that as well...
So please, be aware, for a peace of your mind, that you're in control of your life.
And somewhere over the stars and time, there's the best version of yourself and that's...
...your personal angel.

THE SWITCHER

When the Switcher comes for me, there's a very little chance to negotiate something for myself! And that something means my very own LIFE.

The Switcher arrives in a car, he wears a black suit, hat and a walking stick.

But some say, the Switcher is a woman!

Well, does it matter really?

For me the Switcher is a woman, damn hot dominatrix who runs the best bakery in the world making the legendary apricot doughnuts.

And you, dear reader, pick your deviation!

The mysterious woman in a sexy leather suit emerges during the night and during the day and she doesn't know no mercy.

She'll switch me from life to death instantly!

Once I'm on her list…

Sooner or later, we'll all be on her list anyway!

It's so peculiar how we people rely on this life existence, how we hold on to the things we're familiar with, how we comfortably dwell in our bodies….until our day comes…

Until we can't breathe any more.

And the day will come, unexpectedly, when I will try to breathe in but only the oxygen I'll get in will be the dust of the grey walls around me squeezing me, crashing me, grabbing my lungs in the firmest of grips.
It's said that the worst death is by suffocation.

It's certain that the Switcher will come for me too.
She will switch me from one reality to another…
It's often a painful and chaotic process…
But it's for sure the Switcher will switch me!

I'm sitting in the cinema.

There are just a few more people observing the film.
There's a scene.
It's after midnight.
Empty street.
A plastic cup is pushed by the wind gusts across the road.
A man in the long black coat stands before the church. He smokes. His hat casts an impenetrable shadow over his face.
He shakes a bit. He tries to control it, but a good observer would recognise that the man is shaking.
Black leather gloves shine in the greenish light of street lamps.
First snow starts diffidently flying in the air.
A lonely crow sitting on a fence observes the man.
And the man observes the crow and enjoys his cigarette.
A sudden harsh cry of the crow pulls him out of thought.
The crow keeps cawing at the man.
The snow fall increases in intensity and a haze crawls through the street and sneaks in between the houses.

Out of the white haze emerges a black van silently and lethally.

The rats, that were invisible and inaudible until now, jump out of the bins and make their way through the holes and crevices back to safety.

The man shakes with disgust.

He throws away the cigarette and observes the car stopping right before him.

There is a golden sign on the van:

SWITCHER'S APRICOT DOUGHNUTS
One is not enough!

A black cat runs across the street as the van's door opens abruptly.

The man leans forward unconsciously as he focuses his eyesight or better his nose. The smell is overwhelming, the smell of an early morning bakery, slightly crunchy on top-soft inside-with homemade apricot jam-doughnuts!

A beautiful black hair woman steps out in a sexy outfit. The unbuttoned black fur coat, that touches the fresh snow on the ground, reveals a spectacular view on her physical lures.
A delicious chocolate in luxury packaging approaches the lonely shaking man.
He has never seen such a bakery director.
She holds a box with freshly made doughnuts in her hand.
He starts coughing.
He tries to stop it, but without success and the snowflakes under his black cowboy shoes turn red.
The man cannot catch his breath.
She comes closer to him.
He realises that she holds a cigarette in her hand.

Her long sharp curved nails are painted blood red.

In a slow motion she raises her hand with the cigarette close to her sensual blood red lips.

She smiles softly revealing her perfect teeth. The incisors somehow protrude.

But the man's eyes feel the irresistible gravity and fall down onto her big breasts.

But just for a split second, because the gentleman's heart gets temporarily off the beat warning him about the way he should behave to keep his chances open…

He tries to read her eyes as she observes him.

Women are walking CT scanners.

They know the numbers pretty quick.

BAKERY DIRECTOR
Hi, would you have a lighter?

MAN
Sure, ma'am.

He pulls out a silver zippo petrol lighter and she puts the end of the cigarette between her magic lips.

She grabs his hand with a lighter by both of her hands, because he is shaking.

Her hands are so warm and skin smooth, a pretty pleasant touch.

MAN
What is such a beautiful lady doing in the middle of night here in an abandoned side street of Chinatown?

BAKERY DIRECTOR
Good question.

MAN
Well…

BAKERY DIRECTOR
Well, I came for you.

MAN
Why?

BAKERY DIRECTOR
Because your time is near…
That's why…

The man on the screen is now in a close up shot, he coughs and spits the phlegms mixed with blood.

BAKERY DIRECTOR
It's a long way…
I took some doughnuts for us.
You'll love them.

I got the strange feeling, I try to recall what am I doing for a living?

I have a strong headache.

After a while I realise that I was doing an audition yesterday, for that stupid unwanted role…

I start to feel dizzy and want to vomit. I need to go out, I need fresh air! The fresh cold winter air!

Far away from this old movie theatre. It's hot here and smelly like a dump dungeon where the homeless people hide.

I'm running from the screening room, through the corridor, I feel weak, my heart is beating very fast, I cannot breathe!

The corridor seems to never end!

It's getting colder and colder as I approach the exit door.

Finally I'm outside.

It's freezing and my heart is calming down.

I breathe in the Siberian air with delight.

The winter will be harsh in Chicago this January, the snow storms are scheduled.

My body starts shaking because I was not ready for the first snow.

I pull out a cigarette and light it up using the matches, and I need to use like five or six before I can make the cigarette burn and get some nicotine inside finally.

But already the second puff triggers a cough seizure.

The snow under my feet turns blood red.

I can see a creepy shadow approaching me emerging from the white haze!

It's a man, wearing a long black coat, holding something in his hand.

I can hear a threatening sound as if a scull clicked the teeth.

The stranger wears a hood, his jacket is definitely well worn and he holds an ejection knife in his dirty hand.

The shadow comes closer and whispers: "There's no excuse, if you lose."

My world is shaking and switches into a hospital room!

Where am I?
Monitor beside me is showing the numbers, heart beat….
Ooh…I see, damn, it was just a nightmare!
These are my first thoughts, but I realise I cannot breathe!
The monitor shows that my oxygen level is only 82 percent!
And my heartbeat is 131 beats per minute!
Shit!

The TV is on.
Some documentary about monkeys living in the north part of India in Rajasthan.
The voice over talks something about survival instincts, predators and herd behaviour patterns.
I woke up, heart racing, suffocating, wanting to cough, but being afraid to cough.
Because when I try to cough the phlegm out, it is stuck somewhere along the way to my throat, like the lift in between the floors.
I cannot cough it out and I cannot breathe in.
A pretty dangerous situation.
I get into a panic state, I force my weak body to stand up and try to cough the phlegm out, I'm using all my force. I spit it into a plastic bag.
Yeah, there's some blood too…
I did it!

At least a bit of it.

But now I am unable to breathe, and I'm suffocating.

I grab an oxygen mask, I turn the Oxygen on, almost a full maximum of secure load.

I put it on my nose and mouth and I finally breathed.

I'm standing close to a monitor panel observing my critically low oxygen level and critically high heart rate. "*That's deadly, man!*" I say to myself, standing behind a special elevated table like a DJ.

I'm shaking, breathing, and the numbers on the monitor are calming me down gradually.

The TV is still on and now there is a commercial break:

There's a dancing little green man selling electronics …

"Christmas is Okay Okay, Christmas is Okay Okay"

"Shit!" I spit out.

I can hear the crows behind the window, I can see the occasional fireworks in the black sky. The snow is falling and the flakes are glittering in the light of street lamps.

Christmas is approaching.

Certain death is crawling, slowly but surely. There's nowhere to hide on the Earth.

There's no corner in the world one could hide away from the monster of darkness.

I stand there with the Oxygen mask on for maybe one hour and contemplate: "*Throughout our life we balance on the thin edge between conscious existence and mysterious death. It's just a question of a slight difference in numbers…*"

A blood oxygen level below 92% and fast, shallow breathing were associated with significantly elevated death rates in a study of hospitalised COVID-19 patients, suggesting that people who test positive for the virus should watch for these signs at home, according to a study conducted by University of Washington at Seattle researchers.

This is what I've found online.

I've just woken up from one nightmare to another and it all seems to be so real.

I go back to bed and I adjust it using a wired control.

With the oxygen mask still on, I crawl into that bed.

I am trying to fall asleep in a seated position on a special bed in my hospital room.

I'm unable to sleep in other positions because I start to suffocate, it's painful, my lungs are inflamated. They only work 50 percent!

To be honest, I'm actually afraid to fall asleep.
That woman in a sexy leather suit both attracts me and scares me, she is so dominant.
She wants to kill me, I'm sure of it!

There are few things I'm curious about, how painful it would be on the scale from one to ten.
How would she do it?
What would happen next?
Nothing?
Oblivion?
Eternal sleep?
Heaven or hell?
Other dimensions?
These thoughts are making me uneasy.

I have realised that I'm afraid of death.
It's something I don't know anything about.

And there's another thing, very important, I have still not reached my main targets!

I have tasks to do before I go.

I know that the woman in my dream was the Switcher!

That nurse, what was her name, ooh…yes! Jane!

A tattoo of gargantuan crab on her hand, Covid protection outfit, mask and shield - JANE herself.

She has mentioned the Switcher, as we were talking about life after death…

Jane studies at an occult university in Phoenix, remotely…

I must get away from this hospital room as soon as possible!

"You were a healthy guy, until you got vaccinated!"

This is precisely what the guy in the ambulance car told me…

And the TV bombards us with an aggressive patience and persistence:

Second dose, third dose, boosting dose, antibodies, Covid bubble, isolation, PCR test, Antigen test, lockdown, state of emergency, respirators, protection shields, intensive care, immersion, madness, numbers of vaccinated, numbers of diseased, percentages, comparisons, border closures, travel requirements, Christmas is okay okay…

The nazi elite wants to kill us all!
They've got the robots.
And they've got the Switcher - the collective dream of metrosexuals.

My grandfather, when he got perplexed by some irrational anomalies intruding his ordinary life, used to say:

"Make a shit on my chest!"

Yeah…

And then he made a horrendous fart, which made me and my brother run away.

Our dear grandad loved the beef and poppy seeds, which made inside his guts a deadly poisonous odour.

He loved to tease us, innocent little boys-angels, with his deadly poisonous farts. God bless him.

He did enjoy to torture us.

When our grandad was small boy like us, he was working as a servant of the nazi officers during the second world war.

Not kidding.

And those nazi officers were spoiling him, bringing him the chocolates, sweets and other treats.

I guess, our beloved grandad, a very heartily and funny strong hard working man, the bicycle enthusiast, was hiding something from us.

He must have been a nazi concentration camp guard!

That was to put it all on a light note…

Heil Grandad!

THE ART OF WITCHCRAFT

I was staring out of the window observing the black veins of the city and the immortal statues of the ancient warriors and kings in the Park of the Marksmen.

I was so down, life got me on my knees and grabbed my throat by its deadly cold skeleton hand.

I thought the only way was to jump out of the window.

To end this suffering.

I did what I could and beyond and still I was here broken, staring through the glass like the elderly people do.

Finally I could understand what the majority of people are up to in this life and far beyond it.

To satisfy their ever hunger of the ego.

To satisfy their hunger to excel.

The race is on.

And then the black raven landed on the window and looked me into the eye.

And I knew instantly that I was chosen, selected, by the wizard, selected to join his University.

Why?

We never know why!

It's in the hands of Masters of Higher Purpose.

They hide behind the curtain, pulling the strings.

Some call them the Poppet Masters.

Some say they are aliens…

And there are some who think they are devils from eternal hell…

The bird looked me in the eye and whispered: "Follow me to the castle, follow me my dear Ghost Writer, follow me the Pistolero, come and fly with me!"

The Master will give you the tools of justice, the tools of enlightenment and immortality.

You'll be illuminated.

But before you do so, there is a contract on your table, the contract, black feather and knife…

Cut your vein softly, consider the red liquid dripping out of it as the canon ink, dip the feather a bit and put your signature right next to mine!"

"Yes, that's it…"

"And now, come and fly with me!"

I looked back to check my room for the last time.

My rented room in Krakow in South East Poland close to the border with Czech Republic and Slovakia. The historical city that was the capital of Poland in the times of Queens and Kings.

Papers, documents and technology devices all over the place.

The signs of intensive study and work.

A few computers on the working table, smelly socks on the lamp, a plate with "paczki" (doughnuts) and a cup of hot coffee on the sofa, a lot of cables all over the place.

And when I turned back, I spotted a reflection of myself in the window glass.

I was terrified!

I have seen a raven!

And the only thing I could do was to fly away.

I flew above the city.

At the beginning I felt dizzy and scared.

Then I flew over the countryside, I felt free.

I continued over the airport and I heard shooting from a gun.

One of the bullets hit me and I started falling down.

I have fallen into a forest.

And when I raised it again, I saw the body of a poor bird lying in the rotten leaves in the Park of the Marksmen under my window.

I thought, now I should travel through the tunnel towards the light, but a monster in the long black coat flew to me, approached me and with a laugh he threw his long coat over me.

The dark entity snapped out "Her Highness is already expecting you...".

And we flew through the black circle in stormy clouds.

I knew where we were flying, I knew that the horrible place is designed for those who commit suicide…

A TAXI TO HELL

The whole problem started when Mephistopheles took the wrong bus at the Havirov train station. Havirov is the youngest town in the Czech Republic, solemnly announced in 1955, and it has been designed to accommodate the vast number of coal mine workers in the times when there has been a mining industry boom. The man leaves the building of the train station, built in the Brussel's style of the Sixties. It is essentially a big hall with its front entirely made up of glass. Looking at his surroundings, Mephistopheles gets a taste for cigarettes, but, simultaneously, as he searches in his pocket for his source of relief, he sees that the bus is arriving and, without a single thought, he jumps in. The bus starts to go in a strange direction, definitely not the one that can lead Mephistopheles home, so he knows that he has made a mistake and tries to get out of the bus to attempt to take the right one to get home. He hopes that the bus will stop at its first station, but it does not happen. It turns out to be a route that goes to one of the coal mines in this region, so it takes a good forty minutes to stop. After getting off the bus, Mephistopheles realizes the first return connection is only after eight hours.

'Shit! Fucking hell!' he says to himself, 'Why am I so stupid?'

He looks around, it is a cold autumn day, with leaves flying in the air as if they are kites. He can smell something burning. There is a tall chimney and a factory made out of red bricks, erected high above the greyish landscape. For the miners it is another working day, for Mephistopheles, it is the day of a big return. He has been traveling for thirty years, his mind is empty now. With no desire, no worries, it is just calm and peaceful. Mephistopheles has been through many things. He has been dead, but he returned. He has been hit so hard, but he has always stood up. He has been to heights and fallen down way too many times. He loved and he hated, he desired and he was escaping. He was left alone and abandoned way too many times, so he knew that he had to rely on himself and God only. All he can do now is to spread happiness, fix the problems of others, and make them laugh, whenever he can, and wherever he is let to do so. *But, we all have been through many things, haven't we? One may think her or his troubles are the biggest.* Mephistopheles, after this state of mind wandering, gets a taste for a cigarette. It has been a long time since he has not smoked. He has been on the road for such a long time, moved from place to place, like a voyager, sculpting a statue of his real self, with a hammer and a chisel covered with the blood of his hurt hands and the sand of the deserts. The man tries to light a cigarette, but he realizes that he does not have a lighter, or some matches. Luckily one of the miners is standing a few meters from him, so Mephistopheles approaches him, asking for a lighter. The miner's eyes are black as if he has painted them. His hair is grey and the wrinkles deep, his teeth are yellow from the coffee and cigarettes, and his breath smells of alcohol. He is probably a young man, a husband and possibly a father, working hard, dying too early, like many of the miners. Ultimately, the worker hands him the lighter. The cigarette tastes great to Mephistopheles, and he enjoys every single puff. The world becomes a happier place, at least for the moment. Suddenly the man feels also the need for a paper cup of hot strong coffee, and he looks around. *There, there's the kiosk.* He puts on a pair of dark green sunglasses, and it seems that the world is traveling back to his childhood. A moment later Mephistopheles stands with the cup of coffee and a doughnut in his other hand. *They make the best doughnuts here, not in the USA.* With an apricot jam, one donut is enough if you eat slowly enough and cherish every bite of it.

'Well, I'll need to get a taxi to get home then.' Mephistopheles thinks to himself.

He doesn't need other friends. He has got one best friend and that's enough, that's all. A moment later he finds himself dragging the heavy suitcase across the street toward a small residential area since here there is a good likelihood that there could be a taxi idly standing in a street with the driver sleeping, covered by the newspapers. As Mephistopheles enters one of the side streets and carries his heavy suitcase, he can see a small boy riding a bicycle. He wears a baseball hat with its cap flap low, covering his eyes. But Mephistopheles can see almost immediately he is a Gypsy. There live a lot of Gipsies in this area. They have rather a bad reputation here because they are frequently stealing in the shops and abusing the generosity of the Czech social care system. Personally, the man does not have anything against them, but his instincts tell him to move his left leg onto the gear pedal, move the gear down and softly touch the brake pedal with his right leg. Mephistopheles checks his pockets, his wallet, and his documents. But his next thought is, 'To hell with all the money, with the worries, I've got a gypsy soul, after all.'

The boy arrives and the man asks him, 'Have you seen a taxi anywhere around here?'

He doesn't respond but points up the street towards the parking place. Mephistopheles looks up and really, there is one taxi there.

'Thanks a lot.' the man says and continues to walk across the street.

He is dragging his obsolete suitcase across the pavement, making that typical noise that only the small plastic wheels of the suitcase can make. The sound of the airport travelers. The taxi driver is a woman, and oh, what a woman! With her long, black hair, big breasts, perfectly shaped bum, red long sharp fingernails, and black eyes she certainly is the most addictive girl that Mephistopheles has ever seen. The man asks the taxi driver if she is available to take him home, and, once she says yes, he drags his suitcases into the trunk of a taxi.

'Do you want me to help you with those ones?' the taxi driver politely asks.

'Oh, do not worry about it, I can do this on my own.' Mephistopheles replies with a smile, 'These suitcases are heavy as hell, I wouldn't want you to curse at me while you carry them.' he then adds.

The taxi driver just nods while smiling politely. It is a strange smile, the one that suggests a certain tightness, even coldness. But the man does not notice this, for he is so eager to get home, being hungry and tired after the long journey that has lasted thirty years. Mephistopheles stares out the window, observing his hometown which has never changed in his eyes.

The best city in the world without a doubt, or so he thinks. Well, there's another best city in the world when he actually thinks about it, and it is Casablanca. But the reasons for these considerations are part of a long story, long and eternal. The man enters the car, he throws the small baby toys scattered in the back seats to one corner and adjusts the pillows. But suddenly, as he sits and bats his eyes, he notices that three women are in there with him.

'What the hell is going on?' he asks himself, 'Have they been this fast to enter?'

But there is no time to think, for the taxi driver starts to turn on the engine and drive away. After some moments, the car stops. Mephistopheles looks at his surroundings, not believing that they have arrived so soon. But, looking through the window, he notices that they are in a desolate land, where three strange cars are parked, long and wide like the vintage American ones.

'Weed, the driver needs to buy some weed, but we are lost...' one of the women utters.

Chills are running through Mephistopheles' spine.

'Come with us to the top of the hill, so we can check where we are!' they say.

He does not understand, but he follows them anyway for a strange reason.

He climbs onto the top but when he turns back, they drive away with the man's suitcases.

'Oh my God, what is happening to me? Why am I so dumb?' Mephistopheles whispers to himself.

He is lost, he has forgotten who he is. He starts to descend the hill, and, once he arrives at the bottom, his surroundings change. The desolate land becomes a lovely town, so the man starts to walk through it. A moment later he enters a bar, or rather a cafe, with delicious desserts displayed. The smell of coffee is overwhelming. The man has forgotten the wonderful, strong, and intense smell that comes from coffee. Mephistopheles approaches a lady, who is serving some black liquid in cups that are definitely not coffee.

'May I ask you what is that?' he utters while pointing at the cups.

She stares at him and only now he realises that she has got some strange horns rising from her hair.

The lady starts laughing and she says something to Mephistopheles. But he does not understand a word, for her language seems to him a collection of gurgling sounds.

He only recognises a 'blb', which is a Czech word for 'lunatic'. Scared and bewildered at the same time, he turns around and sees people with strangely red faces and horns.

'Ma'am, could you please give me a bit of that hot black drink that smells so intense and so good?' he tries to ask again.

She makes the strongest double espresso that is available as Mephistopheles searches for the coins, but it seems they don't accept that currency here. So the man takes one of his golden chains off his neck and asks the fascinating lady to exchange it for their local currency. To his surprise, she pulls a small metal box out of the drawer and puts it on top of the bar.

The man is curious. Or lost? Aren't they the same thing after all? Mephistopheles is new to this world as if he is a child, but with an adult's brain. Nevertheless, with a wiped-out memory. *Why did I come here? What the hell am I doing here? What happens next?* The sexy lady opens the box, revealing small red crystals, then she picks up a golden pyramid, and she places a few of the perfectly cut red gems into the holes in the pyramid. Then she hands the pyramid to the man. He stares at the shining exhibit. The bartender nods and hands him over the cup with the black hot drink. He smiles, and she does it back, but they are different kinds of smiles, his is innocent, while hers is seducing, tempting like the devil.

'Helena.' she utters, touching her big breasts.

'Helena?' he repeats to ask.

'Helena.' she nods with a certain tone.

Mephistopheles wants to say something, to introduce himself, but he does not know his name anymore. So, he just smiles.

Holding the cup of coffee, the man walks through the back door of the cafe. To his surprise, the city that stands before him is very different compared to the picturesque town where he was a few moments ago. The skyscrapers are touching the red clouds and some of the buildings are floating in the air. *Maybe I got mad. Perhaps I got lost. I have never seen such a place before!* Mephistopheles feels uncomfortable as he leaves the well-air-conditioned cafe. It is so hot in here. As if he is in hell. To calm himself down, the man sips the black, hot liquid from the cup and he concludes that it tastes great. Suddenly he hears some scream from a distance, coming from behind that hill the girls from the taxi were asking me to climb on. The man runs toward the hill and he walks on top of it to see what is happening. And as Mephistopheles is climbing the hill, the scream gets louder and more awful, disturbing. When the man approaches the peak, his heart races as fast as ever. The moment the man stands on the top and looks down, his heart squeezes in his chest like a lemon.

There is an abyss as if it is a volcano crater, and the bottom is filled with red, hot lava with some people floating in it. They are shaking their skulls and bones, and squeaking, screaming, yelling, crying. The view is terrifying, but the man does not feel any emotions anymore. He finishes drinking the coffee and pulls the golden pyramid with the red gems out of his pocket. In its precisely polished walls, Mephistopheles sees a reflection of his red face, with horns rising from his head. Some signs on the bottom of the pyramid appear as the man turns it upside down, three identical numbers, the sign of his destiny. 6 6 6.

THE SWITCHER IS BACK

A prisoner sleeps on his bed. Well, he tries hard to fall asleep, but his mind wanders into the land called the Past. He starts to cough, firstly sporadically, but then in such an unstoppable and painful way that he becomes breathless. The prisoner keeps changing his position on the bed. It's a hard one, not exactly the bed of a Princess characterized by its seven mattresses, four pillows, and enormous, warm, and thick blankets stuffed with goose feathers. His teddy bear, lying down at the prisoner's side, is a Qur'an, the holy book. The prisoner seems delirious, maybe of the lack of oxygen in his lungs, or perhaps because of all the time that he has spent yearning for freedom and salvation, and as he closes his eyes, hoping to find, eventually, some peace for his soul, he mutters some words, that are uttered like in a prayer.

'I have failed, in everything. I've hurt so many people, I've had so many dreams, but I didn't make them come true. People I love had many dreams, I didn't help them to fulfill them. It's bullshit, that American dream! It's just damn branding, a slogan, a motto... All they want is your money, love, and soul. Slaves! To hell with the elite's mind games! Obey! The residential status fucking game. When the Switcher comes for you, there's very little chance to negotiate something for yourself, and that means that you have to give up your own life. The Switcher arrives in a black limousine, he wears a black suit, hat, and a walking stick. But some say the Switcher is a woman! Well, does it matter really? For me, the Switcher is a woman, a damn hot dominatrix. Are sex and death that close to each other? And why? The mysterious woman in a sexy leather suit emerges during the night, and she doesn't know any mercy. She'll switch me from life to death instantly! Once I'm on her list... oh, but I won't have to wait that long, sooner or later, I'll be on her list! It's so funny how people rely on this life, on their own existence, how they hold on to the things they are familiar with, and how they comfortably dwell in their bodies, until their day comes. Until they can't breathe anymore, and surely then they will lose everything, including their identity, and their perception of themselves. That, my friends, is the real death. And the day will come, unexpectedly, when I will try to breathe in but the only thing that will get in will be the dust of the utter destruction of myself. It's said that the worst death is by suffocation. Well, then rest assured that the Switcher will pour the Sodium Hydroxide down my throat. The Switcher will tear my guts. The Switcher will burst my heart. The Switcher will cripple my mind. Rip my spinal cord off. Cut my head off. Oh yes, there are millions of ways to die. No matter what have done, no matter how much I possessed. No matter what dreams I've had, no matter how much I have loved. No matter how much I'm still hated or loved. Talking about love, why did I make such a mistake, why did I leave her? I wanted to return to her, but she had refused me. And who can blame her? I did cause a lot of pain to both of us. Oh, God, I'm so sorry! The Switcher will certainly come for me, so please save me! The Switcher will switch me. It will strangulate me. And my last thought will be about her, the love of my life. And my last question will be expressed in scant words. Why do we have to go through all of this if all will be lost in eternity? Why?' he says.

* * *

Suddenly a torch casts overwhelming light on the prisoner's face. A figure appears before him, the one of a monster in white protection clothes, a mask, a shield, and gloves. There are the others, surely its followers. The prisoner moves into a seated position, and he sees that the monster is holding a syringe in its hand. The cage bars slide open. Finally, after a few moments of silence, the monster speaks.

'Do you know why we are here?'

The prisoner looks at him, confused and scared.

'No, why?' he responds.

'I'm a nurse from the Trace and Protect Team and I have some questions to ask you.'

The monster walks toward the prisoner, who is sweating and trembling in delirium. He screams as the creature inserts the syringe into his arm.

* * *

Larry wakes up in an enormous room with walls made entirely of mirrors. *Oh, thank God, it was just a dream.* But suddenly his peace is interrupted, for he sees a person appearing in the mirror. Larry is in shock and grabs a handgun.

'Who are you?' Larry asks in an urgent tone.

'I'm your son, Larry!' the stranger finally speaks.

'My son is dead. I'm just sleeping... It's just a dream, once again!'

The stranger looks at him with a compassionate smile.

'No, it's not.' the person utters, as he steps out of the mirror, stretching his right hand,

'Just grab my hand and you'll see it's not a dream.' he, then, adds.

Larry hesitates but then he stands up from his bed, makes a step forward, and shakes hands with a stranger. Larry is bewildered.

'Do you see? I just came to you, to tell you, that everything will get better. That everything will be good, dad!'

Larry shakes his head.

'And how do you know this?'

'I come from the future, I'm the best version of your son, dear father. I could also say that I'm the best version of you. Because of the place, I come from, those two identities are one and the same. In fact, I'm you! Your life on Earth is just a dream and soon you are going to wake up.

But don't worry!

'Don't bullshit me. My life is over and I'm going to put an end to it now. And guess what? After that, there'll be nothing, damn nothing... forever!

'Trust me, I promise you, everything will get better! You're not you, you're not a cop, not a detective, not Larry Fixman. You're me! All will be good.'

Larry raises his gun.

'If you're me, then I'm going to shoot you down, stranger.' Larry Fixman utters, as he points his handgun at his reflection, and pulls the trigger. The mirror breaks and the image disappears, but there are his reflections all around him, so he turns around shooting in a frenzy. All reflections are gone but one. Larry stares at it and searches for another magazine to load the pistol. Nevertheless, the image of a person dressed in black moves toward him. She has long, black hair, hypnotizing eyes that are as black as two holes in space, and red, sensual lips. She looks so beautiful. She speaks, and the sentence seems to evoke a strange emotion inside Larry.

'It's time to go!' she says.

SOLOVKA

A shaky hand places a record on the gramophone and the other places the needle on the groove of the disk. A room is lit by a lamp and one can hear the tones of jazz composition with the smooth and sweet vocals of a lady. There are black and white photos of people on the walls, of a younger man with a girl and a dog; of the same, a little older man and the dog, but without the girl, and the picture of a man alone a decade later. Empty beer bottles are lying down on a duvet, and an ashtray full of cigarettes and joint residues can be seen on the working desk, along with an opened porn magazine. The first snow of this year, illuminated by the street lamps' greenish light, is falling behind the windows. Abandoned, empty bottles lying on the ground, that used to contain wines, such as Châteauneuf-du-Pape, Beaujolais Nouveau, and the likes. They all left an hour ago, but still, some noises can be heard from outside the house. Loudly singing women are walking under the windows, and some of them are laughing drunkenly. The man yells for the last time and there is silence. On the ground in the hallway, next to the door, new fashionable winter shoes are ready, along with a big suitcase. Running water can be heard, followed by the sound of swallowing, and a disgusting burp. Jirka Nowak, a divorced man in his fifties that is very overweight, is sitting in front of the screen computers. He slowly prepares another joint with yellowed fingers. There's dirt behind his long nails. Now everything is quiet as the record finishes playing. Jirka Nowak pulls away from the joint. Everything around is shrouded in smoke, and Novak can only see the dragon statues, the statuettes of an alien and a unicorn, the lonely Buddha bust, a model of a windmill, and old books. The alarm clock shows that it is half past two in the morning. Jirka Nowak is checking his email. On the computer screen, there's a photo of a sexy blonde in a black lace blouse, with her head seductively tilted. The girl has dark, intense blue eyes. Long real blond hair. Full pink lips, calling for a sweet passionate kiss. She reveals her pearly white teeth in a slightly contemptuous defiant smile. Her breasts are big, calling to be grabbed violently, with or without the owner's permission. A large, golden necklace adorns her neck. Jirka Nowak feels that the girl is looking at him. *That she is alive.* He spins around on his turning chair, turning back to face his desk with his stare transfixed on the computer screen. Above the photo of the beauty, there is an email.

'Hello, my name is Elena. I live in Russia. I want to find love, marry, and create a happy family with a loved one. Have a happy future with him, and become his other half.
If you are interested, write to me, I will be looking forward to your answer!'

Elena's sultry eyes radiate the rays of promise. Jirka Nowak plays a Russian song on YouTube. He pulls away from the joint and his gaze turns dreamily to the window, behind which large snowflakes fall down quietly. Light is everywhere.

* * *

Snow, fog, and frost are what is characterizing now the city of Moscow. A black car is rushing out of the big city. Birches line a narrow path along which a small river flows. The car passes a sign on which there is written 'Solovka'. The snow is deep and black. Wild dogs fight with crows for carcasses. Rats feast in scattered garbage cans, licking the remains of sardines in tomato sauce. In the small pond, there is a small ice pool, where the tough Russians swim. Boys and girls play ice hockey. Drunk people, with bottles of vodka, are roasting at the caravan buffet. A hundred-year-old grandmother, hunched down to the ground, is smoking a cigarette. A black cat sits on a rusted tractor. Ravens have a meeting in the treetops. The black transporter stops at a tin cottage. The radio can be heard from inside the car, playing a kind of thoughtful song. The driver gets out first. He is tall and thin, and he is wearing a long black leather coat. Kalashnikovs emerge from under the seats. The man has long white hair and scars on his face, and he has a bottle of vodka in his other hand. A smaller man in a blue and white striped tank top emerges second. He has a tattoo on his shoulders, silver chains around his neck, and sunglasses on his eyes. He pulls out a gun from his pocket, and he slowly pulls the trigger to shoot the last man that is sitting in the car. Tears are streaming down his face, while he is desperately smoking and drinking vodka. On the mirror swings an orthodox cross, and it is attached the picture of a woman. She is a beautiful blonde, with dark, intense blue eyes. The man takes the photo placed in the mirror and looks at the girl.

Outside, some little Chinese kids start firing firecrackers and fireworks. Suddenly, gunshots and yelling can be heard, but everyone brushes it off, thinking that the fireworks probably ripped off someone's hand again. Three men open the back door of the transporter and bring out two black bags. They carry them inside the tin house. Two of the men return and take a large suitcase out of the car, along with a bag. One of the guys checks the badge on the suitcase.

Jirka Nowak
Orechova 13
Praha-Smichov
158 00
Czech Republic
Tel: +420 723 666 254
jirka.nowak666@gmail.com

"Вот тебе любовь, дурачок…" he utters with a smirk.

They drag everything inside the house. The door of the tin house closes with a creak. The snowflakes fly in the storm. Darkness descends on the horizon. The dogs still look back in the distance and their dark bloody eyes glow with hatred. One of them runs away from his companions with a ripped hand in his snout. The rest of them chase him. The sky gets illuminated by lightning here and there.

CLAIRVOYANT FROM AHNENERBE

arl stops in the street to catch his breath, then he runs toward the hospital. He's already flying up the stairs. Then he bumps into the nurse, and he apologizes. The young man stands in front of the doctor, who informs him that his wife has unfortunately died. Carl can't seem to move, so the doctor helps him into the room where his Eleonor lies. Carl sits by the bed on which the sick girl is lying. The girl doesn't move, she doesn't breathe, her beautiful big black eyes are without any signs of life. Tears run down Carl's face as he sits down with a girl who has gone to an unknown land forever, distant from our world. Carl snuggles up to her and cries. The girl's wide-open eyes are fixed on the ceiling. The doctor quietly backs out of the room and closes the door, then he walks with his head bowed down a long corridor whose walls are painted green. There are tears in his eyes. His glasses fall to the ground. He picks them up, blows out the dust, and puts them back on. He walks over to the window. Soldiers stand in the courtyard, smoke, and flirt with the nurses.

* * *

Carl sits at his desk in the room, drinking a hot tea and he generously pours into it some Cuban rum. He looks at the photos in the album. On some, he poses with his colleagues and friends in Nazi uniforms. In most of the photos, however, he is captured eternally with his beloved Eleonor.

He pulls one picture out of the album. He puts it on the table. He lights a cigarette pulls hard, and the smell of burning tobacco and paper calms him down for a moment. An utter silence follows. She is watching the beautiful girl in the photo.

'Perhaps you are in heaven and when my time comes I will come there for you! If there is a paradise where we are eternally young and immortal, please wait for me.' Carl cries.

He opens a wooden box where he stores items and memories. There is a silk orange napkin with the embroidered inscription 'Eleanor' and an imprint of her lips painted with red lipstick. There is a silver ring, bearing an official emblem of Ahnenerbe, the Society for the Research and Training of German Ancestral Heritage. There is a stained emerald ball. Carl takes it into his fingers and has a vision as he measures it in the sunlight.

A little boy rides a tricycle and stops at the bushes where he has built a hut with his girl. She stands in front of her children's home and looks out for the boy. He comes toward her.

'How were you at work?' she asks.

'We had a lot of work, I'm so hungry!'

'Come on, then, I cooked dinner!'

'What's for dinner tonight, my love?'

'Goulash.'

The boy kisses her love, and they both enter the hut hand in hand. There, in jars made of stone, clay, rowan berries, and muddy water are prepared. The kids eat dinner glancing at each other with affection.

'I have a present for you.' the boy begins to say.

'Show me!'

He pulls a colored glass ball from his pocket and hands it to the girl. A smile lights up on her face.

'And you will marry me?' the girl asks with a grin.

The boy simply shrugs.

'I don't know.'

The answer makes her sad. The girl nervously mixes the clay with berries and he throws the ball in.

Carl sits, smokes, and watches the ball as tears drip on the wooden table. The ball falls out of his hand, dribbles on the table for a moment then falls on the ground and rolls away. Carl tries to catch it, but in vain. He runs after it as if it has become the most important thing in the world. But the green glass ball disappears into a crack in the floor. Carl tries to chase it, but without succeeding, for it's gone. He rips wooden boards, but the ball is nowhere to be found. The man, ultimately giving up, sits back at the table and gets drunk with rum. He, then, gets hungry and prepares poppy seed cones, along with a strong Turkish coffee in a tin mug. He has a vision again. He, Eleonor, and his friends dance naked in the wild woods around the flaming totem pole of branches and leaves. Nazi uniforms are thrown around the tree. Utterly exhausted, Carl falls asleep.

* * *

Clouds are rising over Berlin. Carl arrives in a black car in front of a large building on which a red flag with a swastika is moving in the wind. At the entrance, he greets the soldiers.

'Heil Hitler.'

Carl's black polished boots run up the stairs. He doesn't wait for the elevator. He stops in front of the office door as his gaze falls on a sign on which a series of words are written.

Ru SHA
Rasse- und Siedlungshauptamt der SS
SS Obergruppenführer
HEINRICH HIMMLER

Carl knocks briefly and vigorously. Someone invites him to go in, so he opens the door. The secretary greets Carl.

'He's waiting for you!' he says.

117

Carl walks into the office of the SS chief and the Ahnenerbe's founder. He salutes and closes the door behind him. Heinrich Himmler pushes a chair behind a massive desk, then his glasses on his nose, and invites Carl to sit down. He offers him some whiskey from a bottle on the table.

'I'm sorry about your wife. Accept my sincere condolence! It is a great loss for Ahnenerbe and the whole Reich.' Himmler says.

'Thank you, sir.'

'This world is an illusion! We Germans, the whole Aryan race, come from a chosen land a land where we are eternal.'

Himmler picks up a glass of golden liquid as he talks to Carl. Carl drinks his glass to the bottom.

The chief offers him a cigarette, and they both relax.

You know, I decided to lead the whole expedition to the Caucasus.' Himmler begins to say.

'I feel honored.' Carl responds.

* * *

Berlin is plunging into darkness and Marlene Dietrich's singing is coming from a nightclub behind the corner. A black limousine is rushing through the streets of the imperial capital. The trees dance in the red light of the street lamps as Carl and the other men are sitting inside the luxurious vehicle, talking with fervor. A fat gentleman with a beard and sunglasses leans towards

Carl. With a smile, he offers him a cigarette from a silver case.

'You will be shocked by what you will see in the Caucasus!' the gentleman says.

'Our 49th Mountain Brigade has discovered the Wehrmacht near the town of Majkop, something that will trigger a lot of interest!' another man adds.

* * *

Carl and his colleagues are sitting on a military plane, which is ready to depart. A man with sunglasses hands Carl a folder. He opens it and skims through it, showing no signs of emotion.

The plane detaches from the ground and, a few moments later, it disappears beyond the horizon.

It's night time and the passengers on the plane are asleep. Some people walk down the aisle, while countless stars shine behind the windows. But suddenly the plane gets into turbulence.

No one is noticing it, but a glowing object is rolling and glowing on the floor. After a few hours, the plane lands in Abkhazia.

* * *

A military car is driving through dense forests around a lake in the mountains. Carl watches the incredible nature outside the windows.

The bearded man leans over to Carl, saying, 'Mysterious Lake Rica! The water from it is ideal for the human production of blood plasma. We call it the "Water of Life". We drive it in silver

containers to get it to Germany.'

Carl sighs as if he is carrying the weight of the world.

'If only it could bring her life back...' he wonders.

An image of Eleonor walking through the park is suddenly vivid before his eyes, along with the flowers, the nature in blossom, and the love on the wings of colorful butterflies. The bearded man looks at him with compassion.

'Unfortunately, it can't.'

He rummages through his beard and adds, 'But we're not here for that, remember?'

Carl simply nods, and, a few moments later, he notices that a crowd of people is running through the dense forest with torches.

Carl, his colleagues, and the soldiers.

'We'll be there!' a man in sunglasses tells Carl.

Carl takes out a photo of Eleonor from his pocket. He watches it for a moment, then he kisses it and hides it back. In front of the men opens a burned-out plateau on which lays a mysteriously large silver disc. Carl, watching the scene, has a vision.

The place turns into a red desert and in the distance, he sees a red city.

'I see something there, let us see it!' the man in sunglasses says.

They start walking, getting closer to an abandoned building. They enter through a hidden opening and proceed cautiously through a corridor, where there is a heavy door made of stone, without any locks.

'We have to push to get inside, so push!' someone shouts and they all gather in a bigger room.

There, on the ground there is a two-legged creature, with horns on its large head, lying down. Its big, black eyes are dead. Carl stares at the creature, bending down in awe. He touches one of its claws and pulls something out of it.

A man in his sunglasses lights a torch on the object that Carl is grabbing. The colleagues and soldiers are the silent witnesses of the revolutionary event that is about to happen. The object is so familiar to Carl, it's a colored emerald green glass ball...

JAPANESE GARDEN

In the garden under the trees, a meditating monk sits, dressed in orange apparel. There's a stone gate behind him. A blind girl with a cane casually walks by. The morning silence here in the garden is only complemented by the sound of running water, rustling leaves, and tapping sticks on stone tiles. The girl disappears behind a rock, while the monk keeps meditating with his eyes closed.

He has a vision, he is floating in space and he flies quietly below a spaceship. He sees the face of the blind girl in a small window. They both smile.

* * *

A blind girl is crossing a busy intersection in Tokyo when she hears a car approaching her with great velocity.

* * *

The monk finishes his meditation session, gets up, and walks towards the moss-covered stone gate. He sees that doctors in white coats are preparing in the hall. The monk stands in front of the gate, while a nurse carries a blind girl in a wheelchair to the hall.

The monk turns on his smartwatch and programs something on it, while the doctors operate on the girl and insert something into her brain, a chip. The girl, conscious, can slowly see her vision coming to life. Black turns into color, emptiness turns into lines, and it is a thing that has never happened before to her.

* * *

A spaceship lands in a Japanese garden and a monk enters it, with the bat of an eye.

* * *

The girl is lying in the room after the operation and she is sleeping. She has a dream, she is floating in space and a spaceship is flying below her. A monk watches her from his window.

They both smile.

* * *

A monk enters a train, to go to an unknown land. He sits in a compartment and reads a book.

The girl, after a while, also enters it, and she sits in front of the monk. The light of the sun illuminates their faces, and the girl enthusiastically watches the world through sunglasses. Can it be true that she can see again? Surely the light hurts, but nothing is sweeter than to see the world.

The monk is reading a book named 'The Shipwreck', written by Alexey Raven.

'Excuse me, sir, is the book interesting? What is it about? You know, I've never read a book before, I have just started to see.'

The monk smiles, handing her the book.

'It's yours.' he says.

The girl looks at him, wide-eyed.

'But it's not...' she tells him.

'I've just read it, so it does not serve me anymore. Take it, it is my gift for you!'

The girl hesitantly takes the book, flipping through the pages.

'It's a book of stories.' the monk explains.

'Stories?'

'Yes!'

'Which one did you like the most?'

'Um, probably the last one.'

The girl runs her finger down the list and comes across the name of the last story. *Japanese Garden.* The train flies through the landscape as the birds sleep in the clouds.

AL-DABARAN

Aldebaran is an orange giant star, located at a distance of about 65 million light years from the Globe, in the zodiac constellation Taurus. It is the brightest star in the constellation and the fourteenth brightest star in the night sky. The name Aldebaran comes from the Arabic name الدبران al-dabarān and it means 'Follower', probably because it is short in the Pleiades.

The Pioneer 10 planetary spacecraft is currently heading for the star and it should get close to it in two million years.

In an old Parisian apartment with many rooms lives an old teacher of French, Arabic, and History, Bousmaha Aziz Al-Malik. He doesn't reside here all alone. One can find him mostly wrapped around warm heaters with his white cat Mimi, which controls everything with her emerald green eyes. It sometimes seems to Bousmaha that his cat's eyes are dark green and that at night they turn orange as if they are two glowing tangerines. Bousmaha Aziz prefers to spend time in his library in his favorite armchair, and in the fireplace, when the fire is burning, shadows of objects, an old man, and a cat dance on ancient books, while the ceiling is adorned with a beautiful chandelier made from crystal. Occasionally, when the fire in the fireplace burns out, Bousmaha turns on a projector that produces a three-dimensional projection of the starry night sky, plays some calming music, and tries to mimic the scent of nature at night. Then he usually meditates or contemplates Allah and life. The library also has a large tree, whose crown reaches the ceiling. The teacher likes to sit in a meditative sitting posture on the ground, in front of the tree, while Mimi gazes at him. And who knows? Maybe Mimi also meditates when her mandarine eyes turn into two swirling spirals. The man also loves to watch the stars with astronomical telescopes. Specifically, at the center of his interest, there is the Aldebaran star system. He frequently reads scientific publications on the subject, other than informing himself on the Sumerian culture. The latter fact can be deduced by the large map placed on the wall of this ancient civilization, which was born between the rivers Euphrates and Tikrit.

Mimi, meanwhile, drinks milk from a bowl, catches imaginary mice, or watches the man motionlessly from the window ledge. It's early in the morning now, and Bousmaha is praying. The sun rises over Paris as people wake up to their dreams, some with joy and others with slight disgust. Bousmaha Aziz walks down the street to a Morocco cafe, where he allows himself to relish a hot espresso and hot crispy Msaman Marocain. He reads the newspapers about the bombing of Syria, the Islamic State, and Iraq, and he is particularly interested in an article entitled, 'What about Syria?'. A Muslim family is walking around his table at this moment, saying hello to the teacher. One of the children falls into the small street pool and starts yelling, so his father picks him up from the ground. A veiled woman explains something to a child.

The child cries, his eyes wrap around Bousmaha, and observe the silent man. He has a cup close to his mouth and smiles.

* * *

Bousmaha Aziz smiles as he stands in front of a blackboard in the lecture hall of the university.

He gives students a lecture on Sumerian civilization and how they invented, among other things, writing. He has a replica of a table with Sumerian records in his hands, and he calls the students together and describes what is written on the stone table.

'...and this is the constellation Pleiades and this red giant star right here is called Aldebaran. Its distance from our planet is of sixty-five light years and, here you can see something like a helicopter. Well, now that I think about it it seems like a flying saucer, or at least that's what it looks like to me.'

The teacher then enthusiastically explains the theory of the scientists that ancient Sumer, at that time, was visited by aliens from some of the stellar planets of the Aldebaran system, and that they were called Annunaki.

'You see, alien civilization was developing long before ours.'

* * *

Two mysterious men in black enter Bousmaha's house. They are wearing black coats, hats, and sunglasses, and their mouth and noses are covered with a scarf. They enter the teacher's apartment, search through everything, whether it is papers or computers, and they throw books off the shelves and pull drawers off the table. One of the men kicks a bowl of milk. The other examines the Jukebox in the corner as if he had no idea what the device does. The device flashes when the mysterious man inadvertently pushes one button. An Asian romantic song starts playing. Both men listen to the music, while one sits in a chair, the other on the table. After a while, they start dancing and undressing each other. Their style is very strange and moreover, they do not seem human. Their heads are large, their eyes are all black and they have only three fingers on each of their hands.

* * *

Meanwhile, Bousmaha Aziz is somewhere on the other side of Paris, specifically in Chinatown, carrying with him a portable cage from which Mimi peeks out. He walks among the hundreds of stalls. He enjoys some Chinese food, picks up long noodles with chopsticks, and the steam of exotic smells is swirling in the air. He strolls through the crowd of shoppers and watches the bustle. He is fascinated by foreign goods. In one of the shops, he greets the owner. The shop owner takes him to his back office. Bousmaha Aziz hands him over a pile of money and the Chinese man hands him the key and pushes a button behind the painting that is hanging on the wall. The wall separates itself into two parts, showing, behind it, an altar with Buddha surrounded by burning incense sticks. The teacher enters the mysterious chamber and the sophisticated door closes behind him. He approaches a large black object with the shape of a perfect black dice. He pushes his fingers inside the holes of the face of the dice, which, after this, splits into two parts, revealing a lock. Bousmaha uses the key he got from the shop owner.

As he turns his key three times counter-clockwise, he counts, 'Uno, dos, tres'. The man gets dizzy as if he is falling into a whirlwind. The man is excited and shouts, 'Go, go, go, go!'.

The cube starts to drag him inside it until Bousmaha and Mimi disappear.

* * *

The mysterious creatures in black are running through the marketplace. Along the way, they show everyone a photo of Bousmaha Aziz and ask people if they have seen him by any chance. Some show them the way. The apparitions get exhausted and hungry, so they must find some food to eat. In one of the shops, they pull out guns and shoot everyone present there, and they suck from their bodies a mysterious blue energy escaping from them. When they finish eating, they continue their search. Chinese singing echoes around the market, a gentle girl's voice accompanied by Asian traditional instruments. Some folks run with paper dragons and tigers and some shoot firecrackers and fireworks. Finally, the two creatures enter the infamous shop, whose owner gives them the key to Bousmaha and shows them the way into the secret room. The two monsters point their guns at him. They shoot the owner, and, after that, they manage to discover the secret room. They enter it and see a black box closing the door to the altar. They try to open the box in some way but in vain. They beat their fists into the black monolith angrily. The magic black cube suddenly disappears, leaving the room empty. The creatures just stand there with their guns in their hands.

* * *

Bousmaha Aziz walks through the red desert toward the enormous orange sun and a foreign mysterious city rising to the sky, where the skyscrapers are hidden by the emerald green clouds.

'There is one more option! I'm a master of escaping, after all. If I die before she does, I will live in her mind. Forever'

Mimi's cat's eyes glow emerald green in the orange light of Aldebaran. Bousmaha is passing a luminous sign on a floating billboard. The letters are reminiscent of the ones of Sumerian. Suddenly he hears a voice from above, powerful and calm at the same time.

'Welcome back, my best friend Bousmaha! Your family, neighbours, and friends, the whole nation, are already waiting for you at the congregation chamber of the Love Waterfalls.

'Thank you, Almighty Allah, for taking me back to your eternal and beautiful shining land! Jannah!' the teacher utters in veneration. His body disappears into the distance. Bousmaha Aziz Al-Malik is back at home. The humble man who loved his family more than himself is about to reunite with everyone he has ever loved, because they are all here, in Allah's eternal garden.

A man, once an old teacher on the Earth and now a young man here in Jannah again, is walking through the gardens, streets, and courtyards of this magic country and observes the splendour, the smiles of young people, families, and children. All young and beautiful looking, and all wearing golden costumes decorated with perfectly cut gems, that are reflecting love and light. Everything is illuminated by the eternal sun of Al-Dabaran. The man opens the cage and releases the cat Mimi, which turns into a beautiful woman. She has long black hair and dark, shining eyes. Her red costume is decorated with dark green emeralds and white, silvery platinum flowers. They smile at each other. After many lives wearing the different imaginable bodies, tested by the hardest exams, they've finally made it. Now they know that to be together eternally is simple. They just need to love each other unconditionally, and selflessly. They walk hand in hand to the main square, in which resides the Fountain of Life. And there, the Angel, the master Angel of Nature, named Delismen welcomes them, spreading her hands, surrounded by animals Bousmaha knew from the Earth and by others that he has never seen before. They both soar into the air and fly hand in hand among the skyscrapers, like the most beautiful and free butterflies in the perfect structures of love and patterns of nobility. Al-Dabaran is love. Jannah is now their only real world, their only real existence. The rest is just our dreams, whether they are lovely or dreadful. Love never ends there, and Satan has the door closed forever. Bousmaha and Mimi, the two butterflies, swiftly fly, and the sound of Gnawa music provides the best environment for their souls to rise higher and higher, to the absolute ecstasy, normally unreachable but brutally beautiful to chase. Allahu Akbar!

SOOTHSAYER

Will Sinister and Lisa Lick are lying down in a king-sized bed. They're making love, and their bodies are only illuminated by the countless lights of Hong Kong, shining through the glass wall.

Her blonde hair is everywhere, stained with blood.

'So now!' Will shouts.

Lisa sighs, while Will stops moving. He looks at the bedside table, then to the ceiling, and finally to the mirror. Yes, he's a lion. The city's body is made of concrete, glass, and mirrors, while the walls of the apartment room, except for the one made of glass, are made of shiny, crystal-clean mirrors. Through the reflection of the walls, Will can be seen as he raises a big ax. There are fireworks outside, a few rich youngsters are having a party on the roof of the neighboring skyscraper. And with a bang, the little colorful stars expand into the deep darkness of the sky.

The mirrors are now sprinkled with a viscose ruby red liquid, as an awful scream tears the moment of dense, profound silence. Will and Lisa are, in fact, screaming with deadly horror and ecstasy.

'There you go! And you said that you didn't want it...'

Will Sinister strolls through his apartment, observing his collection of various antiques. But let us leave Mr. Sinister to do what he has to do. And now, let us check our hero, Larry Fixman.

Well, a strange kind of a hero, to be honest. Larry Fixman sits in the striptease club called 'Red Heart', residing in the infamous district of Mong Kok. The girls are dancing at the poles, while Uwe, a man from Copenhagen that Larry didn't know an hour ago, pushes various hundred-dollar bills into the panties of hot female students from around the world. Larry and Uwe drink cold beer as they debate online stores. Uwe has a small textile factory in Shenzhen, that produces bathing suits. He came there to check the production, to make sure he is not screwed that much.

Larry, on the other hand, is a private detective. They met at the Felix bar at the Peninsula hotel in Tsim-Sha-Tsui, and somehow they ended up here. Larry came to Hong Kong to look for the girl who went missing. An old case, but by chance, someone dug this out of the dusty piles. Uwe advised him that this club and this part of town were places where young girls, here and there, are getting lost. Larry showed photos of the missing girl anywhere possible, attached posters with his phone number, and stumbled around the city.

Larry has smoked a lot of cigarettes during those two weeks, drank beer, and visited various nightclubs. He has irritated his nasal septum with way too much cocaine. He has lost a lot of money at casinos and brothels. But, at the same time, he kept calling the parents of the missing girl, stating that the cost of the investigation is spiraling and that the city is damn expensive. He has also recently broken up with the love of his life, so he's trying to forget it somehow. In the meanwhile, a few blocks away Will is starting to slice the girl's body. When he is done, he carefully packs everything in black garbage bags, and then he puts them in a large one.

He carefully cleans everything in the apartment and wipes the fingerprints, glasses, and everything the girl could have touched. He, then, takes a shower and put his blood-stained clothes in the washing machine. Will goes through the whole apartment once again and thoroughly checks that everything is right. Satisfied, he approaches the table with an antique gramophone, picks a record, and places a needle carefully on it. A few bits of pleasant scratchy sound and the song starts playing. Will approaches the large glass wall behind which the towering skyscrapers keep glowing into the night. Indian romantic music is played on the gramophone.

'Kill the lights!' Will says, and the apartment plunges into darkness.

The silhouette of Will's body curls slightly in the rhythms of the song. The washing machine finishes the washing stage and it starts to dry.

Will organize the clothes and the sheets, carefully ironing and folding them into the closet.

The music is still playing and Will is now sitting in a state-of-the-art kitchen. He drinks espresso and bites from the croissant with a generous portion of apricot jam. Will loves the latter, especially when it is home-made. The killer gets dressed, and he exits the apartment, dragging with him the heavy bag with the girl's remains across the hall, to the elevator. Then presses the button. The door opens, and he finds inside the elevator a young couple. Everyone is surprised. At this time of the night, it is rare to see someone. But Will particularly enjoys taking risks, so he pulls the bag inside with him. The elevator door closes. There is music there, a quiet jazz melody with Indian elements. They're going down. Will measures the lovers, glancing sideways. A Chinese couple. The next time he should invite a couple. The girl is very sexy, wearing a miniskirt and gold bracelets adorn her long hands that are embracing a young man. The latter, a young flamboyant man, has one hand tucked in the pocket of his jeans. His detachment ignites a playful flame inside her. They are obvious under the influence of alcohol, so they ignore Will and start kissing. Will stares at the big bag with the sliced blonde model and slightly smiles. It's his typical dreamy smile that gains the hearts of people. After all, he's a politician, not just an ordinary murderer. He's far away from California, from his very own Beach Town. But here he can fulfill his filthiest desires, in this concrete jungle, under a fake identity.

* * *

Larry Fixman, his new friend Uwe and an African woman with never-ending legs stagger out of the club. They say goodbye to each other, all in a pretty drunken state. Uwe calls a taxi and leaves with the black woman. So Larry is left alone in the night. He wanders through the streets, which are empty in the morning. He meets a Filipino prostitute, who lures him into the dark alleys of sex. She is scantily clad, her big breasts are plucked from a leather vest, and one of her dark nipples peeks out. Another prostitute in a miniature leather skirt pulls him into a dark alley in a haunted courtyard.

Larry pushes her eagerly against the metal wall. Indian romantic music comes from afar. But suddenly the face of the prostitute turns into one of his ex-girlfriends, who has recently broken up with him, and the two find themselves in the shower on a beach. Larry takes off her swimsuit and makes his way to the unknown mystic lands. Their naked bodies shine beautifully in the light green lamp.

'Here?', she protests but she doesn't actually mean it.

It's the plan of the night. Larry is unstoppable, as the ocean rumbles behind them. They don't mind the mosquitoes flying around at all. They do not exist for them.

Mosquitoes are hungry, but the two are even hungrier. So much blood is pulsing in the heated bodies. But Larry suddenly feels a sting in his back. His ex-girlfriend suddenly turns back to being a Filipino prostitute. He is drunk, so he does not notice it and rips her panties down. She clenches her long, dirty nails into his back under his leather jacket. They're in a dark subway, once again. Her face is scarred and rough, and her teeth are yellowed, yet she looks sexy and looks like a goddess of sex. She unbuttons his pants and whispers in a drunken voice, 'Money first!'. With one hand, she pulls the wallet out of his back pocket. While he kisses her on a dark neck covered with stains and tattoos, she tries to examine the contents of that wallet.

It's empty, except for tickets, an Octopus card from the subway, photos of some girls, and then Hong Kong dollars.

'I have nothing, you bitch! I lost everything in the gaming machines! But the money will be, they'll... I'm looking for one... I'm a detective ... I'll send money... I'll pay later... oh, you're so beautiful...' Larry growls in an extremely drunk voice.

She tries to push him away, while Larry feels the sting on his back again. He turns around and a huge Arab stands behind him, but Larry can't see his face in the glow of the greenish light.

The world is spinning around him. He falls to the ground between black bags, leftovers from restaurants, dead rats, and rusty microwaves. He sees only the silhouettes of a pimp and a prostitute walking away through the streets.

'Hey! Wait!' Larry moans.

The prostitute turns and growls, 'No money, no sex!'

They disappear around the corner in the streets of Tsim Sha Tsui.

Larry touches his back and feels something sticky on his fingers. He looks at them, from which a copious amount of blood drips. Now he feels severe pain in his back and abdomen, both covered with red fluid. As Larry tries to raise it, he stumbles and one of the black plastic bags opens wide, revealing its content.

Larry freezes. Dumb blue eyes stare at him from the black bag. The man pulls a photograph out of the pocket with a painful grimace on his face. He compares the faces. *Yes, they look alike.*

He has found her, at last, but not in a desirable state.

* * *

Larry sits in an Indian restaurant as he enjoys lamb on spicy curry with rice.

'Damn, I have to lose a few pounds' Larry contemplates as he tries to think of what to say to the poor girl's parents.

The detective pulls the photograph of the girl and observes it. He gazes into the past.

One day I'll be history too...

'They will need to identify the remnants, hopefully, they will at least stick the body together.' Larry thinks to himself, glad the local police will administer that gruesome session at the mortuary.

Larry grabs a napkin and with disgust, he dries up his forehead and cheeks. His attention is caught by the television screen.

'Why are sex and death so close to each other? They're like eternal lovers.' The beautiful ladies in exotic costumes sing as they dance. It is a typical Bollywood production, but what is not typical in Larry's eyes is this hotness. The fan rotates above Larry as he stares out of the window. It is four o'clock in the morning, yet everything about Hong Kong seems so alive.

BEACH TOWN

Maria shut her windows and pulled down all the blinds. Outside, the weather was still fine and calm, but she didn't care. She felt someone was out to get her. What she didn't understand was why it had to be now, after all these years.

She sighed when her eyes caught the framed photo of a younger version of herself with a fine young man.

'How time flies,' she muttered.

She fell for the sofa without turning and collapsed into it. The framed photo was clasped tightly between her palms like a prayer book. Her eyes were firmly shut as memories of life before Beach town came rushing back. Something she rarely allowed.

Clips of her dancing with her mother in her father's lavender field in Lavender bay whirled around in her mind. She could hear her laughter ringing above their heads. Her father had stuck out his long arms with bulging biceps in awkward angles while dancing and her mother made a face.

Her mother always brought along a basket of carefully packed lunch whenever they went to spend the day with papa in the fields. So once they were done with harvesting the spice and having a little fun, she spread out a cloth on their favourite spot and began unpacking the sandwiches and muffins.

She remembered her mother, holding her hands firmly but softly, telling her all the reasons why snatching a sandwich before the grace was said was punishable.

'It's just you screaming 'no manners' to everyone you are dining with.' Her voice was clipped with anger.

''Is that what you want to tell people?' She asked.

Little Maria quickly shook her curly blonde hair. She knew better than to disagree with her mother.

Life had been perfect with her parents before the spice market crumbled and the both of them turned beseeching eyes to her. She was pretty, young, and healthy so she could at least marry one of the rich youngsters who sought her hands in marriage.

'Papa will be able to start again with the money from your dowry.' It was her mom speaking and watching her intently. Most times, she felt her mother's eyes following all her steps, waiting for her to fall so she squeezed her prim and proper lips in disgust and sigh.

Maria was not ready. She felt too young to venture into something as serious as marriage. She pleaded for a little time at first. When the time was up, she panicked and pleaded for more, and more, and more. She was just 16.

Soon enough her mother was staring at her with eyes that looked like steel.

'You do want us to survive these hard times, Maria, don't you? She was plucking the little girl's eyebrows and dabbing her cheeks with rouge. Another suitor was on his way and she had to look perfect..

Her accusations started out as seemingly innocent questions. But she lost her patience quickly and the question marks which served as cloaks for her mean words were tossed aside.

The depleting resources at home made it worse. Papa went from calling her sweet pet names to screaming her name with so much force that she'd jump in fright. She had to make up her mind about one of the young men quickly.

Maria settled for the man with the most dowry to offer her parents. Alaine was his name and he wasn't much of a talker. The week after the wedding, she packed her precious belongings and left his house. He was gentle, and kind, but Maria knew it wasn't her life she was living and she couldn't continue.

Beach town offered the most anonymity while she was still on the run, and that was why she decided to settle there. The people asked no questions. They didn't want to know and she loved it that way. Four towns before she got to Beach town, she had heard the owner of an inn whisper to an attendant that the sheriff said to look out for a distressed young lady.

She didn't care to hear more. She entered her room, shut the door, clambered down from the window and continued her journey. By the time the sheriff and the innkeeper forced her door open the next morning, she was already three towns away.

Beach town was not like that. However, something else was wrong here, she just couldn't place a hand on it. Sometimes it was the fact that everyone had the same dark expression on their faces, gloomy faces that reminded her so much of her mother.

Other times, it was the way the townspeople huddled in two's and three's while saying nothing and staring into space that unnerved her the most. They seemed to speak with their eyes. Something she couldn't understand even after three decades in their midst.

She had started a bakery two weeks after she arrived with the money she stole from Alaine. A small concrete affair where she made and sold breads, cakes, croissants, and pies. It didn't bring her closer to the people as she thought it would, but it gave her enough money to provide her needs. They always came with the exact amount of money they needed, pointed at what they wanted, paid for it and left. Even the children kept quiet when she tried to initiate pleasantries.

When the weather changed drastically two decades after she settled in Beach town she tried her best not to mind much. The constant wind gales and tornadoes caused more harm than good to the town, but how could she complain when the townspeople went about their businesses like it was normal. Once, after the roof of the bakery was blown away, she found herself in front of the town council building the next morning.

The sheriff, a big dark-haired man with bushy eyebrows and hooded eyes, stared at her for a long time before he said anything. When he finally opened his mouth it was to grunt that 'orders have been given.'

She left more dispirited than she was when she came. She was astonished to see the roof neatly nailed back when she returned.

The bakery got better, but the weather kept changing for the worse. Worst still, whisperings of strange sightings flitted past her ear every now and then. A ghost in a black cloak, houses that were hunted, and a sand spirit that moved with the wind. She never saw the faces of the whisperers, but she always heard them when she walked through the dark narrow passage that ran in-between what would have been known as the poor neighbourhood if only Beach town folks cared for class.

The stories caused her goosebumps and made her close the bakery earlier in the evening. The people didn't complain. They began buying things earlier. She was happy she didn't have to suffer financial loss, but deep down her pile of antagonism towards them got bigger. Maybe she would have felt better if just one out of all the people that dropped in for baked goods asked her why she had to close earlier. No one ever did.

Maria closed earlier like every other day and left the bakery. She smoothed her curly blonde hair with its streaks of grey and held it at her nape with a pale red ribbon. It was among the things she took from home which she still had with her.

She left her apron on because she preferred the colourful pattern to that of the plain dress she had under it. She had gotten it at one of the three identical dress shops in the town. Apart from being identical in structure, the shops sold the exact same things. Plain ugly dresses with similar drab colours. She'd never understood why they sold such dresses.

She marched briskly through the empty streets with a warm loaf for her dinner held tightly under her armpit. There were no whispers floating into the streets from corners today. A gust of wind blew, raising sand and dust as it passed. She ducked her head, squinted her eyes, and walked faster. She wanted to be cosily tucked in at home in no time if a storm was coming.

Her house, a small brick building at the end of the last street, was already in sight when the wind started again. It howled fiercely and filled the air with dust and sand. She dashed for her house with all the strength a lady in her mid-forties could muster. The howling intensified as she frantically searched for her keys in her apron pockets. Somehow the wind sounded like the plaintive cries of an old woman to her.

'Where are the damned keys for chrissake!' she whispered furiously to her self.

Just then another gust of wind swirled around and her door creaked. Her hands paused midway through their search and grabbed the door handle. She turned it and it gave in. Her jaw dropped, she could swear she locked the door before leaving in the morning. The storm forced her into the house, lots of sand was coming in through the open door.

She jammed the door shut and leaned on it for a while before flicking the switch. Bright white light flooded the room. She took a cursory glance of the room to make sure everything was in place. Satisfied with what she saw she exhaled. Inside the safe brick walls of her house, she knew and felt her safety was guaranteed.

'You can howl all you want outside,' she was talking to the wind.

A strong gust of wind blew outside and her doors and shutters creaked and slammed. The brick building vibrated causing a shiver to pass through her. The wind heard her. She shook her head.

'It's just one silly storm.' She shook her head again to clear all the creepy stories she had heard from her mind.

'Beach Town is my safe place,' she whispered to herself. She repeated it as she changed from her apron and dress to more comfy house dress. Dinner was forgotten the instant she sat on her bed.

She kicked off her shoes and snuggled under the warm covers. Even the storm was forgotten.

She just got back from the bakery like every other day and let herself into the house. She was not alone, someone was banging pots and pans in her kitchen. She grabbed the closest thing to her, the coat hook that stood behind the door, and took tentative steps towards the kitchen. Her jaw dropped when she saw who it was.

''Mother!'

The silver-haired woman looked up and clapped her hands in glee.

'Alas, my town pumpkin is finally back from work.'

'How did you find me?' She asked.

'You thought we were searching for you?' she chortled.

''How mighty you place yourself, my little princess.'

'You weren't looking for me?'

'Tut tut tut, why not just shush and come enjoy this sumptuous dinner I made for us. It's been so long, my little Maria.' She peered searchingly into her daughter's eyes as she made the last statement. Maria shuddered a bit.

She knew that look from all those years ago. Her mother had not forgiven her after all these years.

'I'm sorry, mother,' she ventured in a squeaky voice.

The older woman cackled and brought down the pan in her hand on the counter with so much force.

'Hold it!' She screamed.

Maria flinched. She couldn't hold her mother's gaze. Her eyes looked like a storm was brewing behind them.

'Hold your half-assed apologies let me show you why I came.'

She lifted her hands above her head and clapped. Thunder struck and lightning flashed through the room and she grinned.

'I'm one with the storm and sand now.'

'Mother?' She took one step backwards and the older woman took one step towards her.

'You are not scared of your sweet mother, are you?'

Her gnarled outstretched hands made Maria recoil. She took a second step backwards.

'Whaaaat is wrong with you?' She was screaming as she made for her daughter with a pan held high in the air.

'I took care of you!'

'I loved you!'

'Even more than I loved my own self!'

'But all you decided to pay me back with was sorrow!'

A storm had started outside, and claps of thunder and streaks of lightning punctuated her mother's words.

Maria was crouched on the floor beside the sofa with her hands raised to protect her head. She might have fought back if it were a stranger, but it was her mother. And even after 30 years away from her, she still didn't have the nerve to fight with her. She screamed as the older woman brought the pan down on her head again and again.

She shot up from the bed with a start. Her hands unconsciously went to her head. Apart from a throbbing headache, she was completely okay. She took in deep breaths to steady herself. It was just a dream.

Her stomach rumbled and she remembered that she had skipped dinner. She stretched and switched on the bedside lamp then pushed the sheets aside. She was going to get herself some dinner.

She was chewing slowly on a piece of toast while thinking about her past. She had never paused to think before fleeing from home, never thought about going back to see her parents. Beach town had had her hooked right from the start. She imagined going back to her parents. What was she going to tell them? Were they even still alive? A shiver of wind passed through the room.

'I'm one with the storm and sand now.' It was a barely audible whisper.

Maria dropped her toast and bolted from the dinning.

'You are what?' Her voice was as shaky as her hands.

'One with the storm and the sand.' The voice was an echo that came from all directions.

She screamed and ran into her room.

'One with the storm and sand!' It was now a chant that got louder with each repetition.

'Stop!' Her index fingers were plugged into her ears.

'Please stop, I'm so sorry I left.' She was crying profusely now.

'Hold your half-assed apologies let me show you why I came.' It was an echo that reverberated through the whole building.

Maria screamed in horror. Her dream was coming true. Something was going to beat her to death with a frying pan from her own kitchen. She looked around the room frantically for some seconds before dashing for her front door. Her shaking hands made opening the door much harder.

'You are not scared of your sweet mother, are you?'

She screamed as she felt the voice directly behind her. The door finally gave in and she ran into the howling storm which drowned out her cries. In the eye of the raging storm, the chant intensified, repeating itself over and over again.

'One with the storm and the sand!'

'One with the storm and the sand!'

'One with the storm and the sand!'

The night left the people of Beach town with a dead body which they found the next morning. It was the baker. The sheriff came with the mortician to the passageway to take the dead body away. No one knew how she got there during such a storm. Her eyes were wide open in horror even though her body was stiff.

The people concluded that she must have seen something that terrified her to death, no one could prove otherwise so the story became true.

EXTRACTION

A low metallic whine sounded as the barrier generator powered down. The faint blue shimmer that surrounded The Grove faded away, leaving the elite enclave of villas exposed; it was officially a part of the conflict zone. Uneasy silence and calm permeated the small area in stark contrast to the sounds of war a few kilometres away.

"This was fast tech work; they're teaching security cracking to basic recruits now?" the extraction team commander commented.

"Call it a hobby, Rick. I'm betting on these skills to get me a real special ops placement when I graduate next year." replied the young-faced soldier, cracking a slight smile.

"It's Commander Rho in the field, don't forget it's a privilege to be brought along on a real extraction mission for an X0 like–" all nine squad members felt the earth shudder. The commander noticed the telltale red beams of light from one of the invaders' Directrix satellites, sliding in a grid-like pattern across the landscape towards The Grove. "They must have noticed the barrier drop from the sky. Triggerman bots will drop here as soon as the satellite confirms the opening; let's move." grunted the commander as he turned and began walking into the neighbourhood.

The villas grew more opulent as the team crept deeper. Some of the properties had their own smaller barriers, somehow still running despite the nationwide power outage. These homes housed the country's ruling class: old money, government councillors, arms developers, and the like, the kind of people that can afford a hundred million credit "donation" for a personal government extraction team. "Who are the objectives? Intel wouldn't tell us who during the briefing." asked one of the team members in a coarse whisper through the comms. The heads-up display of each soldier's helmet showed a small overhead map of The Grove as well as a compass arrow that pointed towards the target location. In the bottom left corner, a line read "SECURE OBJECTIVES: 3." The squad was nearing what looked to be a cul-de-sac—the marker on the map pulsed at its far edge. "It shouldn't matter to you; we have our orders, lieutenant. To avoid any confusion, I'll tell you the targets are Jane, Caitlyx, and Adstra Banis. The Director considers them max-priority assets to be secured out of the country at all costs. Their extraction takes precedence over all of us making it back safely." answered the commander, seemingly agitated by the question.

"Banis… Titus Banis of Banis Exotech? The corporation that produces the weapons we're carrying and the barrier generators they're using to isolate slums? It doesn't make sense why the Director would give us specific orders to–" the young-faced soldier added before being interrupted by Commander Rho.

"I already said it doesn't fucking matter why. We have our orders. Without Titus, this war might already be over." spit the leader.

The team had made it to the gates of the only house on the cul-de-sac, a lavish villa that could have contained ten of the properties they had already passed. A mountain of glass blocks and steel beams, even in the dark, the place shone like a habitable diamond. A familiar blue shimmer shrouded this property, too. Unprompted, the well-trained team fanned out into a wider formation as they approached their destination. The commander tapped a key on his bracer, switching comms channels, and muttered something inaudible to the rest of the soldiers; the blue shimmer dissipated, and the gates opened. "Give me a break; this is not what I signed up for when I took that academy pledge to defend the people of–" the sound of concrete buckling killed the budding argument. Metal cubes the size of bears fell from the black sky and slammed into the driveway, both in front of and behind the approaching extraction squad. Each Triggerman buzzed to life as numerous red pinpoints of light appeared on their surfaces, and they began to rise, suspended in the air a half-metre from the ground; the dots swirled and moved in irregular, unsettling patterns. Without wasting a second, the machines began their attack. Each swirling dot of light emitted rapid pulses of energy, sending lightspeed projectiles toward the soldiers. They immediately broke formation as each person dodged in different directions. All of the initial shots were stopped centimetres from their bodies by automatic bursts of barrier energy made by their personal equipment systems. One of the combatants drew a handful of silver spheres from a belt pouch and lobbed them at the line of bots between them at the villa. Moments before impact, each sphere broke open, spreading white-hot needles that embedded themselves in the hulls of the machines. The needles found their precise targets, piercing most of the lethal red lights. Shooting from a handful of remaining dots, the hobbled Triggermen continued their assault, though now with less speed and force. Commander Rho dove forward from the ambush volley, rolling between two of the front bots. He remained kneeling and attached a device from his vest onto the toe of each of his boots. The devices looked like two black metal spiders with deep red LEDs on their bodies. Rho began to ascend the driveway, crossing the pavement at incredible speed like an ice skater. His gliding steps left two lines of molten hot pavement in his wake. "Commander, what are you doing?" shouted the young-faced soldier. He tackled a fully functional Triggerman with his shoulder, knocking off its alignment and causing it to propel itself into the street; the hideous cube collided with the slate retaining wall that encircled the grounds. "It's ten-on-eight here without you. What are we supposed to do?" The commander did not reply. Each remaining soldier heard a familiar chime in their earpieces: the notification of someone disconnecting from the comms channel. The leader resumed his ascent. He reached the towering glass door and shattered it with a swift kick. Commander Rho entered the house. "Are you kidding me…?"

THE BIG CATCH

There was no big catch since the accident, the seas no longer gave him the same joy they once did. He was left hollow by guilt and regret for the boy who died before his eyes.

The sun crawled onto the roof of a wooden cottage. A young couple and their dog lived here by themselves. A cool breeze brought the salty air through the trees and into their windows.

"Ector? Hello?" His wife said, waving a hand in front of his rugged face. He was caught in a daze for the same reason every morning. Outside, a wooden cross marked his son's grave. It was the first thing he would see. A reminder of his mistake, watching him for the rest of his days.

"What is it, dear?" Ector asked. "You've been staring at him again. You didn't know there were sharks. It was an accident, alright?" Glancing at his hands, he couldn't help but blame himself. "I keep thinking about how different things would be if he was here, Mona. If I wasn't such a coward."

An old dinghy was tipped on its side by the front door, covered in years of algae. The names Ector, Mona and Lear etched into its hull. A Golden Retriever slept soundly in its cosy footrest.

"We can't keep going like this. Living off what little you find in the lake. What about our future? What about-" Mona stumbled on the couch. The world spun around her. Ector moved to catch her as she continued. "I'm okay. Please, dear. Will you head back in the sea? For us."

"No. I can't. We'll do just fine the way it is. You'll see." He held both of her hands together on his own. "Today will be different. I promise." "I'll be back by sunset. Love you!" He packed his equipment—spears, bait and a sun hat— and headed out. "Whoops. Almost forgot." He bent down to pet their dog. "Morning, Riley. See you later."

Gallant Lake was downhill from their home. Schools of carp and chub came in from the waterfall and out the river on the other end. Ector was the lone fisherman of the lake, yet he spent his days chasing stragglers by the docks. Earning the bare minimum for their next meals, and little else. Crates and baskets littered the wooden platform. Empty and unused, save for a few. A rocking chair beneath tree shade and a bucket of mackerel for bait.

Some time later, a familiar scent had caught his nose. The deep sea made its way into the lake, carrying a large box. It followed the current from the river, but there was no place it could have gone adrift from. Bride, the closest town to their isolated forest haven, was miles away to the north. Someone was nearby, but they were not from the island. The box was of Buloke wood and high grade steel, sealed with a thick lock. Whatever was in there, its owners had a fortune to spend on keeping it locked up. It could be gold. Jewellery. Perhaps long lost treasures uncovered from a Viking shipwreck off the coast. Its pungent musk grew heavier as Ector drew close, coming from dark liquid that dripped off of the opening. Treasure could not leave a scent as strong as fish would. A trophy from the depths was his best guess, but the box's make was overkill for transporting a dead fish. Ector could leave it alone and move on with his day, but what was man if not a curious creature?

He spent hours chipping at the shank with rusty bolt cutters. A thrill of adventure for the first time in ages. He placed his hands on the heavy lid, but a gunshot bursting through the air nearly blew his hand off. A man appeared from the brush, covered in scars, blood and filth, and a finger itching to fire another shot of his Martini-Henry. Screaming at Ector in a language he did not speak.

"I don't mean any harm, sir. Just a humble fisherman." Ector said. Behind a crate in his path was his harpoon gun, out of sight from the stranger. Both of them had one shot to end the other. Raising his hands behind his head, he continued approaching the stranger. The stranger screamed even louder. Unable to get his message through, Ector threw a basket as he rolled for his harpoon. On instinct, the stranger fired at the basket, and a pool of blood soon formed around his feet from the metal tip lodged in his lungs. A fatal blow.

"I'm sorry." He said, closing the stranger's eyes as his own widened from the realisation that he killed a man. After a closer look, Ector did not recognise him as one of the locals. The stranger had crossed the sea. What made him so desperate to chase this here, he wondered. There weren't many sea creatures nearby that needed a box of that size. A basking shark, bluefin tuna, sunfish, giant oarfish, and a few more, yet none of these were close to the truth. A little girl in silken cloth, buried in dirt from the chest below. He fell on his back as he gasped. Death was nothing new to the old man, as the sea held its grip on many of his friends, but seeing a child—another child—dug into the scars in his heart. Not a fish or fine jewellery. It was her who smelled of brine and seaweed.

But for a drowned corpse, her face should not look as good as it did. Unless…

Ector felt a pulse run up her neck. The girl was unconscious, but still alive. He rushed her home.

Between his breaths, he said, "Mona, dear! Get the first aid kit!" Riley ran to the bedroom when he heard his master's voice, but growled upon seeing the girl. "Hey! She's a guest, buddy. Calm down." He pulled Riley away when he started barking at her. He was brought outside, and ran off into the trees. Ector didn't bother following him. He would come back on his own. Mona covered her mouth. "Oh my god. What happened to her?" Ector told her everything that happened by the lake. The stranger tried to kill the girl. That explanation was what made the most sense to them. He was lucky he found her before the stranger could finish the job, though they could not figure out who she was.

Mona tended to the child as Ector had not reached his quota of fish. Walking through the forest, he heard Riley crying. Ector found him leaning on a tree stump. Dark green blood on his teeth. The dog bit into a toad that shouldn't be there. They didn't live anywhere near the area. Riley was too weak to get up. His heartbeat slowed down. "No… Damn it." Ector stroked Riley's head as he held his dog close to his chest. He couldn't bear seeing him in pain. Ector stood by him until the end. "It's okay. It's okay. I'm here." Back at the docks, the whole lake was emptied of fish. They gathered by the waterfall, trying to swim upstream. It was the biggest and easiest catch he had ever seen since moving to the lake. Even his days at sea would not compare to these carp spiralling into each other as if they were sardines. They weren't salmon or trout. Carp had never done that. His bait bucket fell over, and the mackerel flopped not towards the water, but away from the box. Ector inspected it once more. He wiped off the dirt covering the top. There were markings scratched into the wood. The size of a lion's claw, or bigger. Not something a little girl's nails could've dented the box with. That is, if she was just a little girl.

Ector ran back home. He made a mistake. The girl wasn't kidnapped. She was being contained, and he had let a monster into his home. He scoured for a knife in the kitchen. "What's wrong, dear?" Noticing the weapon in his hands. "What are you-" "Out of the way!" He said, pushing her aside. His hands were trembling, questioning if this was the right decision. He stabbed the girl, but grazed her bleeding skin as Mona held him back. "Are you insane? She's a child!" "She's a monster!" Ector knocked her across the room. He hoped he was wrong. He hoped he would end up a murderer rotting in jail as he thrust a knife into the girl's heart. The knife hovered over her chest, inches away from her skin. Her eyes were wide awake. She flung the knife away, along with the sound of thunder ripping through the air. Heavy rain blackened the skies. "Ector…" Mona called out, blood dripping from her hands and the knife in her gut. "MONA!" Ector reached out to her, but was thrown crashing through the wooden wall and next to his son's grave. He was covered in mud all over. A fog blurred out his house even though it was at such a short distance. A dark silhouette of the girl shifted before his eyes. The girl was no more. In her place was a monster coming at him. Now the size of the box he found her in.

Iridescent gills shimmered in the faint light. Barnacles covered her grotesque blue-skinned body. Her hair grew out into a snow white mane. Jagged teeth lined her slithering tentacles. He was overcome by fear. Frozen in place. There was nowhere left to run from a fiend that shapes the weather. The monster waved its hand, and each raindrop swirled into a sphere around Ector's head. Making him lose consciousness as the monster watched his delightful irony. A man of the sea, drowning on land. Ector searched his surroundings for anything to fight back with. The soft soil had loosened its grip on the wooden cross. He hurled it at the monster, striking its shoulder with an ear piercing shriek. It was unable to slay the beast, but the pain it felt was enough to make it lose its concentration. He tackled the monster back into its prison. It flailed and slashed at Ector, leaving cuts all over his body. He sealed it shut with a fishing spear. Ector fell over, exhausted, but it was not time to rest yet.

"Mona! Mona." He held her up. She was pale, sweating and had her clothes drenched in blood. "Ec… tor?" "Shhh. Stop talking. I-it's gonna be okay." She held his hand, then led it to her stomach, saying, "Peggy. That's… our daughter's name. I wanted to… surprise… you." The light in her eyes faded away. "Mona? Hey." His tear-soaked hands trembled on her shoulders. "Stay with me. You stay with me. No. Please. Please." He screamed as loud as he could, clutching her cold, lifeless body in his arms. He tucked her in bed one last time. Gripping another fishing spear, he said, "Good night, my love." Ector walked outside to check on the box, but it had disappeared from where it was. The winds blew it towards the lake. The monster could still move despite being contained. He dragged his boat back into the water and tossed the stranger's rifle inside. In less than an hour, Ector had lost everything he lived for. His dog, his wife, his home, and his unborn daughter. There was no life for him to leave behind. Nothing but vengeance was on his mind. He would hunt the monster down, or die trying.

A few days later, the box washed up across the sea. A young man approached it, curious as anyone would be. He grabbed onto the spear wedged into where a lock was placed, about to pull it out when a gunshot bursting through the air nearly blew his hand off. A man appeared from the brush, covered in scars, blood and filth, and a finger itching to fire another shot of his Martini-Henry. Screaming at him in a language he did not speak.

THE LAST STORY

The sun's shining through a tangerine sky with long, soft rays as it is setting, its reflection on a large, crystalline lake whose waters are moved by a gentle, warm breeze.

A fisherman is on his small wooden sailing boat, coming back to shore with a net full of plump fish, tired after a long day. As he comes to the lakeside, he notices a peculiar object on the ground. It is a golden pyramid with a ruby embedded in the centre of one of its faces. Absorbed by curiosity, the man studies the object, touching attentively the gem, coming to push it slightly.

The pyramid vibrates as it sucks the fisherman in, without leaving any trail of his existence.

Close to the shore of the lake, Beach Town's habitations stand, illuminated by the gentle sun. The village, hugged by massive mountains, is composed of small, well kept houses positioned neatly near its stone streets.

Diomede is going to the shore of the lake to do what he loves the most, which is to swim through the fresh waters to refresh himself. He reaches his desired place through a small, pebbled street and afterwards he dives into the lake. The feelings are indescribable: the water cleanses Diomede's head as he feels renewed. He swims on his back, admiring the incredible blue, violet and peach of his view, while his ears, underwater, hear the closest thing to silence, something comparable to floating in space. After an indefinite amount of time, Diomede realises that night has come, and that he should probably get home. He swims back to shore, and suddenly notices a faint glimmer near him. He walks towards it and observes that the object, illuminated by the moon, is a pyramid made of some sort of metal, decorated with a precious stone.

Intrigued, he picks the pyramid up, observing it. But by an unfortunate chance, the boy does the same thing that the other poor man did. He disappears beneath a silvery glimmer. Subsequently he immediately finds himself launched in another dimension, surreal and idyllic. An immense desert stands before his eyes, with pyramids placed irregularly on it. The sky's rose coloured, with white clouds decorating it. A gentle wind blows, bringing along sand, colouring the air golden. The place seemed archetypical, as primordial but simultaneously as present as time itself. But then Diomede notices that somewhere in the sky there's a black crevice, spreading disease to the landscape.

The young man's too absorbed in admiring the scene to realise that he doesn't know where he is, or how to come home. All of a sudden a hooded figure appears before him, his face hidden by shadows.

"Who are you, mortal?" asked the mysterious figure.

"I simply am what you've stated, a mortal" Diomede answered with wide eyes "who are you, I must ask?".

The individual sneered. "I am Nathrengar, the Shield of Darkness.

I ruled the world, spreading violence and darkness until hundreds of thousands years ago, when Surys, the Sun you see each day of your life, decided to persecute me. Rather than become a prisoner for the rest of my eternal existence, I chose to run away. I was a wanderer unable to practise my magic for all of these years, until I found, in a ruined, remote palace, a Pyrames, an object who can transport you to Arches, the abandoned reign of light, exactly where we are right now, and let you hide from whoever you want.

Here I could practise my powers and, as you can see, they are working the way they are supposed to. Soon I'll kill Surys and bring destruction upon the world, for it to come back how it was. Are these enough particulars?".

Diomede keeps staring at Nathrengar in awe, unable to move.

"Well, if you haven't got any questions I must take my leave". The Shield of Darkness turns away as he vanishes.

"No! Wait! What am I supposed to do here?"

But no voice responds to Diomede. Dejected, he starts to wander through the desolate land. Minutes, hours pass without noticing any difference in the place or in the time. Diomede starts to worry about his life: for how long could he keep going in these conditions? But then he begins to see the desert quickly turning to prairie, and then to green, luscious fields, flourishing with colourful flowers and a fertile river, as if he entered another dimension.

Diomede keeps walking until he trips onto an undefined item. Wondering what it is, he turns to notice a stone medallion laying on the grass, marked by odd, mazy patterns. The young man tries to pick it up, but it seems attached permanently to the ground.

He traces the carved motifs with his fingertips. "I should try to press this" Diomede thinks to himself, not having anything to lose.

Light liberates from the edge of the medallion, blinding him. Strange whispers fill his ears as he spins around. Hearing a melody, his vision focuses on a luxuriant rainforest, prospering with life. Before him stands an altar made of trees, where sits a woman, the most beautiful that Diomede has ever seen: with a skin of the colour of silver, she's dressed in a green, long gown and her delicate features convey a vigour he's never seen. Little and big animals surround her, enchanted by her crystalline voice. The woman notices Diomede's presence, stops her chants and smiles, almost relieved. "Oh, I've been waiting for you! Let me present myself, I am Delismen, otherwise known as Mother Nature. I'll say this rapidly, Surys, and all of us, really are in extreme danger. The apparition that you've seen before plans to kill the Sun, and you well know that without the Sun everything perishes, including nature. The world will become cold and ghastly, but you can prevent it. You must have come here through a Pyrames, and bringing a human here is detrimental for the Realms in which you have walked, for it shifts the energies within ourselves, blinding us all. You found the Pyrames so easily because of Nathrengar's will, that's unmistakable. So here's what you must do." From her hand a stone medallion, almost identical to the one used to enter this Realm, appears. She blindly hands it to an intrigued Diomede, who takes it quickly, almost excitedly. "This will be your way home. You shall match it to the one that you have used to enter this Realm, let Surys do the rest, before it's too late.

With a single blink, Diomede finds himself transported back to where he was before. Suddenly his eyes focus on a figure, specifically a man. Once Diomede recognizes him, he starts to run towards him. "Dan! Gods, it's so good to see you, I cannot even describe it!" He hugs Dan tightly, allowing himself to release the fear built up in the last lapse of time, which felt infinite. "Diomede, don't ask me, I've been wandering here for days...". Dan says, hugging him back. "Now we have a way home, though '' Diomede affirms "follow me".

The two men stroll towards the embedded medallion. Diomede quickly takes the other one and matches the patterns of the medallion that he has to the other one. He pushes it slightly. Light sets free from the medallion, transporting them back to Sunfall. They appear on the shore of the lake, and what greets them is not home, but destruction. The sky's complete darkness dominates the scenery before them, with the faintest hint of a sun ray, the last one. Destruction lays upon Sunfall like a hurricane. Men, women and children are running away with desperate agitation without knowing where to go. The air grows thick and cold, colouring itself with a red hue. The moving torches are the only thing illuminating the streets. Darkness seems to form monsters that could kill them all with the bat of an eye, while homes are being emptied and burned to light up the surroundings. Diomede and Dan run towards the village. Between all the chaos the fisherman manages to ask a fugitive woman what has happened.

"Dan! Diomede! We were so worried about your disappearance! It's been one day since we last saw the sun. It's terrible, as if these are the last seconds of our lives! Oh, gods! We will never see light again!" The woman shouts, the mob flashing between them. But then something happens. The lone sun ray's light intensifies, just to be joined by another one, and then the infinite amount that we are used to seeing. The light, slowly but unrelenting, absorbs the chaos of nothingness, enlightening everything. The pitch black of the sky's replaced by a serene blue. The wind, finally blowing, extinguishes the torches. Stars appear with their sister, the moon, and a colourful aurora is painted on the atmosphere. The Sunfall's inhabitants admire the peaceful spectacle, calmed, with a smile slowly forming on their faces. Diomede and Dan observe the scenery, mesmerised and relieved.

Later in the night, everyone goes to sleep, either in the remaining houses or camped outside. But Diomede does not. He runs back to the shore of the lake, hoping to find the Pyrames. When his eyes discover the golden object, he lets out a breath. He carefully picks the pyramid up, caring about not pressing the gem. With every force that he has in himself, he throws the Pyrames in the lake, hoping that no one will ever find it again!

A MESSAGE FROM BEACH TOWN

Fear, if there was something I knew well this was it. I could see it in the face of every person I met on the street. I could perceive it even when people smiled. Oh, I knew fear like I knew my own shadow and it had been like this since I had been given birth to. You would think that as a town near the beach, Beach town would be full of smiling people who lived a slow life. It was the opposite, even though people smiled in favour it was always strained because they never knew what could happen to them by the next minute. My parents told me that there was once a time when it was not like this when people did not perform their every duty anticipating that they may lose their lives the next minute. If there was ever a time like that then it must have been before our Mayor Sinister became mayor and he has been mayor for as long as I knew. The mayor was paranoid and believed everyone was after his position, whenever he felt that there was a threat to his power (even though this threat is imaginary), he went on a rampage, kidnapping people and killing people. He controlled everything going on in the town, every single thing. Why had we not reported to the federal government so we could get help? Well, the mayor got some tech experts within the town to create software allowing to access all messages and calls that went through every person's phone in the town. Those who attempted to report were silently killed. Everyone learned to live quietly to save their lives.

I was the only child of my parents and had been careful to keep my nose out of trouble. However, I could not keep ignoring the unbearable shadow of fear cast over the beach town. It was stifling, I could not say what I wanted to say, and even when I followed every rule the mayor may still decide that he wanted to destroy me and get away with it. I had to do something about it, this was my senior year in high school and it seemed like the perfect time to work on the plan that had been growing in my head for months. I was lost in thoughts on the step-by-step plan for getting rid of fear in Beach town when I heard my mom call loudly.

"Andrew! Andrew! Come downstairs this instance!"

What could I have done wrong this time?

"Yes, mom"

"What are you doing in your room?"

"Stuff"

"What exactly is stuff, Andrew? You stay holed up in your room barely coming out to eat. You've not eaten anything today! Yet your grades are going down and you tell me you are doing stuff. Stuff!" She let out an angry laugh

"Mom, I'm eighteen. I have some things I would rather keep personal. I am not just wasting my time, I have plans for my future and I have to work on them from now"

My mom scoffs "Plans, you have plans. All you do is type away on your laptop from sunup to sundown. What exactly do you call those plans?"

I looked at my dad for help, he locked eyes with me and shook his head, I was on my own. I looked like my mom in every way, with her brown hair and green eyes but I had my dad's temperament, I hated arguments.

"Ok mom, I'll work on my grades and try to eat more" I rubbed my forehead "Is that fine?"

Her breathing slowed, she blinked twice before replying "Yes, yes that's fine"

I rushed back to my room, I had so much to do but I kept getting interrupted. My mom did not believe I had plans, my plans were going to shock her and save Beach town. I started this project last year after my best friend was kidnapped for no reason but bad mouthing the mayor. He was never found and I had concluded that he was dead. I was creating software that could bypass the mayor's software, send messages and delete them with no trace. It had been taking hours of coding and had failed several times. I had adjusted it again and hoped that this time it would be successful. At night, I had finally finished setting up the software.

"Please work, please work, please work"

I typed out some words and sent a message to my phone. It worked! It finally worked! I had been able to find a way to send a message to the world outside the beach town without getting caught. The next step was to send the message to the Federal Agency for Human Rights Protection. I found their mail and number months ago but could not send a message because I had not finished the software. I immediately sent a message with the full details of the kidnapping, murder, and corruption going on in Beach town. I had set the ball rolling, I only had to sit back and enjoy the show.

I thought a federal agent would appear in no time, especially with the urgency of my message, yet I noticed no one appeared. What if the message was not sent? I checked again to be sure and saw that they must have received the message. I could not focus on school, I kept wondering when the federal agent would arrive. After a week had passed, I was sitting in the local cafe, matching on a doughnut when I saw a black sedan park. Our town was small enough for me to know when a strange car appeared and this was one. I stood in a hurry, hitting the table beside me.

"Sorry," I said to those on the table. They looked at me like I was weird, well I had not felt this excited for the past eighteen years of my life. If this was the federal agent then things were about to get interesting in Beach town. The car door opened and a lanky man stepped out, he did not look like the picture of the federal agent that I had in my head. He looked completely innocent, maybe I had got my hopes up for nothing. I walked closer anyway trying to figure out if he was who I was looking for.

"You're new"

"Am I that easy to spot?"

"Should I answer that or was that a rhetorical question?"

He had a silly smile on his face "please do"

"Your car, this is the first time I am seeing it here, second you kept looking around as you came down from your car like a tourist who was trying to figure out a new environment, third you are dressed officially on a Saturday morning, should I go on?"

"No, you must be really observant"

I shrugged, I was already disappointed that he was not a federal agent.

"So, what brings you to our small town?"

"Come closer" he waved me over, I looked at him strangely but curiosity won, so I drew closer to him. "I am a federal agent, I came here to investigate the mayor"

I looked at him bewildered, was he joking with me, or was he actually a federal agent. He did not look like one, he did not act like one and he looked like someone the mayor would get rid of in a minute. No, no, this could not be the federal agent or else there was no hope for Beach town.

"You are not saying anything" He was still smiling "Let me prove it to you" he brought out his ID. This was really the federal agent, this was the person I spent months developing software just to contact. To say that I was disappointed was an understatement.

I groaned. "You are the federal agent?" Is a federal agent supposed to be going around telling everyone who he was? I thought they were like spies.

"Yes, I am" His expression changed to a serious one. "I only told you that because I know you were the one who contacted us. We traced where the message originated from and found out it was from you. Please tell me that this was not a prank?"

He thought I was pranking him and that was why he put on the act. Now I could understand him.

"No, it's not"

"Nothing in your town looks like what you described. I drove around already, talking with some of the locals and nobody supported what you described."

"They would not explain what is going on to a stranger, anyone who does that could be kidnapped"

He still looked unconvinced "How do I know that you are not spinning tales? I never wanted to be on this case"

"Give me a week, just a week. If you find out that what I said is true, you will help us out."

"If not, I could have a well-deserved vacation in Beach town," He said, replacing his playful mask. Judging a book by its cover was a real mistake.

"So how do you plan to convince me in a week?"

"Follow me"

I had to get him inside my room without letting my parents know. Luckily they were not home, still, I rushed up the stairs dragging the federal agent with me.

"Hey, what's your name?"

"Fixman, Larry Fixman"

"Nice name, can you fight?"

"Why do I need to answer that?"

"Sorry, it's just that you don't have too many muscles and well we might need fighting skills"

"I can fight kid"

"Alright," I said, raising my hands in surrender. My room was upside down, papers littered everywhere, and clothes were all over my bed. Mike raised an eyebrow.

"Sorry, I wasn't expecting a visitor" I cleared the only seat in my room and gestured for him to sit. While waiting for him to appear, for the past few days I had been gathering information about the mayor and his operations. I handed over the file to Larry.

"Ever since I was a child in this town people went missing with no explanation and never appeared back. Many people lost family members and friends and even though it was not said out loud we all knew that it was Mayor Will Sinister that was behind it. Then about a few months ago my best friend Ace in anger said some negative things about Mayor Sinister. He disappeared the next day and has not been found till today. We live in fear in Beach town, we have no freedom because all our messages are accessed by the Mayor and those who work for him"

"Then how were you able to send that message?"

"I had to create a software that would block their access to my phone for a few minutes while it sent the message and then delete the message before restoring their access. That was the only way I could send it without getting caught."

"Can you show it to me?"

I did, his eyes looked bright now as if he was excited "okay, you have me convinced but we cannot do anything about Mayor Sinister except we catch him doing something wrong."

"Oh trust me something will come up soon. At least one person goes missing every week"

His eyes widened, "it's that bad"

I nodded "meanwhile, while we wait, can you get casual clothes to look more like a local and hide your car somewhere so that people will not suspect you. We don't get close to outsiders in Beach town because we fear the wrath of the Mayor"

"Why were you talking to me in public then?"

"I took a risk and I can say that it was worth it"

Larry got a hotel to sleep in and did his underground research trying to find evidence of the crimes of the mayor. He was working tirelessly but he could not find much. The mayor always cleaned up well after himself and everything that could implicate was wiped fast. I met with Larry to plan how to go about investigating since it seemed none of us was making headway.

"I have never struggled so much in researching a case. There is absolutely no information on this case at all."

"I have not found anything too but maybe that is because we are looking for videos or audios instead of targeting witnesses."

"Witnesses would not want to talk and ruin their lives"

"Yes, no one would want to talk except if they have nothing to lose"

"Which means we might not be able to find anyone to witness for our case"

"That leaves us with one option, we become the witness"

"What do you mean?"

"We would have to go undercover"

"I like the sound of that"

Larry rolled his eyes "Trust me, it is not as fun as it sounds"

"If you say so"

We spent the next few days tailing some of the mayor's men. When we finally figured out their daily route we prepared to knock them out and make use of their uniforms. Larry was making me run every day and it was stressful. I get back home and nod off to sleep without giving it much thought or effort. On one of those days, while we were jogging, a very pretty lady jogged past us and waved at us with a smile. I was immediately suspicious but Larry was not, he beamed enjoying the attention so I decided it must be my bias towards pretty ladies that were at work. We met her on our morning jogs every day from that and she kept approaching us trying to create a conversation. Larry was a goner but I kept having a nagging feeling that something was wrong. Why was she always on our jogging route when we took a unique route? Why did it seem like such a pretty lady was chasing Larry? Something just did not add up but I kept ignoring it seeing it as a bias. We moved on with our plans and knocked out two of the mayor's secret agents at night, we exchanged clothes and tied them up. We were fully kitted in their black outfit and looked every bit like them.

We entered the mayor's house with their IDs and immediately started scouting for where they kept their files, Larry had warned me to not make it obvious that we were looking for anything so we greeted the other workers like we were part of them and out of the corner of our eyes we kept looking. We were aware of the CCTV in the house so we paid attention to acting normal. We finally found a room filled with computers and files. The problem was how to enter without allowing the CCTV to see us.

"How are we going to enter with this CCTV?"

"Just watch my back"

"Alright"

He walked to the blind side of the CCTV while I kept watching. He brought out something that seemed like a spray from his back pocket and sprayed the camera. It was frozen.

"How did you do that? That is so cool"

"Please act normal, there would be nothing cool about losing our lives"

I lost all excitement at that point and we entered the room with the files. Immediately, I started working on the computers while Larry kept watch. I had already worked on a way to open the computer without a password. Although it took a few minutes, I was able to unlock the computer.

"Are you done yet?" Larry asked

"Of course not"

I brought out the flash drive and began copying everything on the file system. Immediately it was done copying the files into a flash, I signalled to Larry. That was the exact time we heard some voices coming down the hallway. I was panicking, if we got caught I was sure that that would be the end of our lives. Larry quickly dragged me behind one of the file shelves that was a bit dark. I could only pray that the workers would not get to our side for any reason. They entered the file room and immediately started work on the computers. I held my breath. I was not sure if I had shut it down.

"It looks like I forgot to shut down the computer," The first person said

"That is a dangerous mistake. If one of the mayor's supervisors were to walk in before we did. We may not be alive to talk about it"

"This is the worst job anybody can have. Every mistake could lead to death. There is no day that I am not afraid"

"Hey, stop complaining, what do you want those who are working as his bodyguards or his secretary to do. One wrong word or action and their lives may be gone"

"True"

We stayed hidden for more than 3 hours, my body was already aching. Larry looked like he was comfortable. I could never get used to small spaces. After 3 hours it seemed they were finally ready to close for the day. They stepped out and locked the door. As I heard the click of the key, I looked at Larry.

"How are we going to get out of here?" I asked

"Stop worrying, just stay calm"

We waited for a few minutes before Larry started working on the door. Luckily it was one of those old doors so Larry could pick it up. On getting home that day I had to work on my breathing to calm myself. I had started this journey thinking it would be fun to bring down the mayor, it didn't seem so fun anymore, I could have lost my life.

The next day I hurriedly went over to Larry's hotel with my laptop so that we could check the information together. I didn't expect to meet him with the lady that was always jogging with us.

"Hi, Larry," I said

"Um hi Andrew, so this is Idara and she'll be working with us"

The lady smiled and stretched out her hand and I shook it trying to maintain my calm. What was wrong with Larry? I knew the lady was pretty but that should not be enough to jeopardise our plans.

"Larry, can I see you outside for a minute?"

"Yeah sure"

How do I convince him that something was up with that lady? I had no idea.

"How can you bring a total stranger into our plans without getting my consent?"

"I didn't think I needed your consent, I am the federal agent here. You are only helping me do my job"

"Really? And you are saying this just because of a pretty girl who paid you a little attention. Can't you tell that something is off about her? How did she know our jogging route and why did she appear every day we were there?"

Larry rubbed his forehead "Look, Andrew, I didn't mean to be offensive but I am not doing this because she is pretty" I raised my brows "She has a brother who was also a victim of the mayor's wicked acts and he is crippled because of that. She wants revenge on him and she is willing to help us out."

"Alright"

There was nothing more I could say. We immediately started work on the files. I spent time sorting them out. He kept a detailed account of his corruption and all the funds he embezzled were spelled out. Even records of the people he killed or tortured were in a file although it was encrypted at first and it took a long time to finally open. I was uncomfortable with Idara around but there was nothing I could do. By the time I was done with the files, it was already night. I stretched out and called out to Larry.

"I'm done with the files, you have all the evidence you need to arrest the mayor"

"Great! Well done Andrew and thank you. I couldn't have done this without you"

He looked over the files and kept working on the laptop.

I packed my backpack ready to go home.

"This is a reason to celebrate, why not stay for a few minutes while I get us something to eat? I'll place an order."

That was not a bad idea, I needed to be compensated for all my hard work and food was not a bad idea. Larry closed the laptop and was working on his phone next, he was so quiet that it got me worried.

"Hey Larry, when would you be taking the flash to the federal agency?"

"Tomorrow seems like a good time"

Idara looked like she was busy ordering the food. We heard a knock at the door.

"Are you expecting someone?" I said to Larry.

"It must be the food I ordered," Idara answered. She opened the door to reveal not a delivery person but the mayor himself and his bodyguards. We were in trouble, even if Larry could fight, how could he take on all these men. Larry did not look scared, I was terrified.

"I heard you were looking into my matter", the mayor said with a sick grin

"It is our duty to bring justice to corrupt public officials like you"

Mayor Sinister's face immediately turned red and he signalled his men to capture Larry. Larry said he could fight but I wasn't expecting much. He threw a punch at one of the bodyguards while kicking the other. It seemed he could really fight but the bodyguards he was up against were too much. Idara watched with a smile and walked over to the mayor's side. That was not a big surprise, I already knew something was off with her. Larry was already struggling and breathing heavily, he moved back and whispered to my ears.

"One, two, three"

Why was he counting? More people appeared behind the mayor. We could not possibly fight ofc this number of people but instead of fighting us, they fought the bodyguards and arrested the Mayor and Idara. What was going on? I looked at Larry

"I called for reinforcement since morning"

"Why?"

"Immediately Idara approached me. I knew something was wrong but I pretended to fall for her story. I knew it was only a matter of time before the mayor was aware of what we did so I reached out for reinforcement. Thank God they came in time I couldn't hold them off for much longer"

Larry had deceived me too, I had no idea he had called for reinforcement and that he had already sent the files to the Federal Agency. Mayor Sinister was arrested and convicted of murder and embezzling public funds and for the first time, Beach town no longer struggled under the shadow of fear. Larry invited me to join the federal agency when I was done with college and my parents finally understood my plans.

THE SWITCHER STRIKES!

A strike of light enters the darkness of the sky. Larry Fixman drives through the desert while he seems to be observed by the palm trees and passes a sign on which it is written 'Welcome to Beach Town'. The sea is uneasy tonight and its rolling emerald waves, announce an upcoming raging storm. A first lightning bolt cuts the tree into halves just right beside the road, and it casts light onto a photograph swinging from the rearview mirror of Larry's car.

There is a happy family in the picture, made of Larry himself, his wife, and their only son.

Suddenly the lonely driver hears a voice.

'Over Here!' it says.

He checks the rearview mirror right when another lightning tears the night. He can swear that he has just seen a monster with the head of a hyena and its snout wide open, revealing sharp and deadly teeth.

'Over Here!' Larry hears once again.

He slows down his car as he passes a billboard, then he stops the car fully on the side of the empty road and turns off the car key to switch the engine. An empty silence follows as Larry stares at the window, hearing the thunder rip the silence apart. A silence follows once again, and only the sounds of the screaming seagulls compete with the rumble of the rolling waves.

The man in his late forties steps out of the car approaches the billboard and lights up a cigarette.

He observes the swaying palms, his golden brown car, the man on a billboard, the sand, and the violet clouds signalling that the sun is about to rise from the snow-white pillows positioned on the horizon. Larry taps on the door of his car as if he is contemplating. Then he opens the door and enters the car, searching for an object. After a while, he emerges with an instant camera in his hand, since photography is his hobby. Larry throws the half-burnt cigarette into the sleeping sand below his feet and starts taking photographs, collecting them in his albums. The man takes one photograph of the billboard and prints it out. The poster consists of a picture of a smiling Will Sinister, a candidate for Beach Town's mayorship, under which there is written 'I'm the Beach Town!' Larry drives his car away from the Beach Town.

He arrived a month ago, but now when he's on the run. He doesn't feel well, he doesn't feel well at all. He passes another billboard with mayor Will Sinister on it. Larry slows down a bit to read the slogan. *Why did you kill him?*

Larry continues, but then, as he spots a figure on the road, he stops his car. It is moving. Is it an injured animal, perhaps? Larry gets out of the car to check it out.

He walks slowly with a grimace on his face. Yes, it is an injured squirrel. He squats to see it more closely. The creature has its eyes open wide and breathes fast.

'I didn't kill them.' Larry weakly utters.

Suddenly a car approaches Larry and the man looks up. It's a bakery car, the one he has already seen a few days ago. And the same lady steps out, looking sexier than ever.

'It's you again...' she speaks with a rough, luring voice.

'Yeah.' Larry responds.

They both stare at the squirrel.

'Let's move it to the side to the edge of the forest.' Larry proposes.

'Yeah,' she nods, 'Good idea."

They find a way to carry the wounded squirrel to the edge of the forest on the tree branches.

'You've wounded yourself!' the bakery director-lady says with worry in her voice, "Let me check-'

'Just a few scratches, here and there, it's no big deal.' Larry murmurs with a tired voice.

The woman comes closer to check Larry's wounds. Blood is everywhere, both on his clothes and his hands.

'She looks so beautiful, Larry thinks to himself.

Everything about her is mesmerising. Her black eyes, her long hair of the same color, her red, full lips, her curves. She moves with elegance, smooth like a cat, like a predator. As if she is on the hunt, all the time. Funnily enough, he barely sees her as she comes into intimate proximity. He can only smell her perfume, a very strange one, but still sensual.

She comes closer and closer until her lips almost touch his. Larry realises he feels both excitement and fear. But soon it is all replaced by sadness, for the woman whispers to him, 'So, tell me, Larry! Why did you kill him?'

Tears run down Larry's cheek, glittering in the cold sky.

'It wasn't me!' he shakes his head in disagreement.

'I know your secret. I know the secrets of all mortals and immortals.' she says.

'Who are you?' Larry whispers, with pain in his voice.

'Do you need to know that?' the woman asks.

Larry now sees the lady has got a white and blue mask on her face. The man grabs it and puts it off. He sighs with relief, there is the beautiful face of his femme-fatal staring at him.

'I thought-' Larry whispers.

'What?' she whispers back and touches his lips with hers in a soft, fleeting kiss.

Then she moves down his face with the little brief horny kisses to his neck.

'I thought...' Larry murmurs again in painful, sensual agony.

Larry can see that she is wearing a black lace eye mask and her breath is hot. So hot he can barely hold himself together. Her sharp long fingernails scratch his face.

'I know it wasn't you, in fact it was me.' she whispers softly. A sudden gust of wind shakes the trees and their squeaking noise welcomes the lost souls strolling the night forest.

Larry screams and pushes the lady away. He touches his neck in disbelief, a lot of blood is sprinkling from his neck vein! Then Larry looks up.

'What the hell...' he only manages to utter, noticing that the woman's features have changed.

'Who are you?' he sighs, struggling to breathe.

A woman with the face of a hyena jumps on him and bites again and again and again.

'I love you! I love you so much that I want to eat you my dear!' she says in between the bites.

She tears his flesh and veins, licks his wounds, and giggles with pleasure. She screams in ecstasy.

Her teeth destroy his face, changing it into an unrecognisable mass of red flesh. And when the beast finishes her dinner, she walks back to her car.

She smiles as she glances at the sign on the door, on which it is written 'The Best Doughnuts in Town!'. She taps on it with her sharp, lethal fingernails and she opens the door.

The squeaking noise echoes in the glittering sky. She checks her makeup in the rearview mirror, as she turns on the engine. The car moves along the zigzag road deep in the forest. The tall pine trees and old oaks are the silent witnesses of all things, whether they are mortal or immortal. The lost ghosts stroll through the darkness and hunt those who are still alive. While the Switcher keeps switching from dark to light, and from light to dark. If we knew, that dreams are reality and reality are dreams, we could carry our love with us forever, and the pain would be gone.

But because the switching system is so well elaborated, often painful, and horrendous, it feels as if one is in a slaughterhouse, being the object of the beasts' appetite. The evening haze falls onto the road as the black bakery van makes its way to another pray.

THE BEST FRIEND

Larry sits in his favourite arm-chair, sips a hot black coffee and smokes a cigarette. And yes, there's a bottle of good whiskey on the table, half-full.

The man looks tired, exhausted, sleepy.

He's a federal agent, he is pissed off of his life and he is expecting a call.

Obviously, very few people know about the fact he is an FBI man.

But we can see his opened badge on the table.

His hand gun is resting nearby.

The cigarette smoke creates a dense curtain, behind which there's only death creeping.

The phone rings and Larry puts it on a loudspeaker.

Larry mumbles "Hi there…".

There's an apparent lack of energy in his voice.

"Hi, is it Larry? This is Aneke from Partnerships Solutions Charity in Durham."

There's plenty of power in the caller's speech, but Larry needs to increase the volume because there's noise coming through the windows. It's the noise of the morning city. Larry lives in ChinaTown, which is adjacent to downtown Chicago. His small first floor apartment is located on the corner of West Alexander Street and South Wentworth Avenue, which is a busy vibrant place day and night.

"Yes, Larry Fixman." answers the muscular man in his mid fifties.

"Great, Larry, as I've said, I'm Aneke from Partnerships Solutions Charity in Durham and I'm running the seminar that we have scheduled with you for today."

"Yeah…" utters the sleepy man in the armchair and lights up another cigarette with a lighter. He looks pretty bored.

"As you know, I believe, this seminar was ordered by the Chicago police district A1 as a part of conditional caution because of domestic violence abuse between yourself and your partner… Are you aware of that?".

"Yea…" whispers Larry ominously.

The man stretches his legs and pulls from the cigarette.

Then he holds it for a moment in his lungs and releases the big clusters of smoke with relief.

Aneke continues "This workshop consists of two sessions and you need to take part in both of them. Should you skip one, the police would take further actions against you, because to attend both telephone meetings with me is conditional caution. Do you understand, Larry?".

"Yes, I do!" answers Larry.

"Anything that you will say during the sessions with me stays confidential, just between you and me." Aneke adds.

"Sure!" utters the man in the armchair and his gaze falls onto the painting on the wall. There's a vulture with an emerald green eye staring at Larry. The vulture looks like Aneke, sitting on the tree branch. There are rusty wagons on the abandoned railroad in the background. *"Everything is confidential…"* contemplates the tired man. He has heard too much bullshit during the interrogations and he has said the very same thing as Aneke way too many times. The history repeats itself again and again, it's like a rotten wooden mill wheel that keeps spinning in the dirty water - in that shit - that flows from the myriads of households of this windy city.

"However, there's one exception to the confidentiality rule. That is, if you would say something, during our sessions, which would make me feel that you or someone is in risk or danger. On that occasion, I would need to notify the police."

"Is that clear, Larry?"

"Yes, it is."

"You'll hear me typing as we'll go through the two sessions and I'll explain to you why. There are two reasons. First, I need to remember what we've discussed today during our next call. Second, I need to show to my manager that I'm really working and not just chit-chatting. Is it OK with you, Larry?"

"No worries. Sure."

"Now, are you somewhere nice and quiet, do you have your privacy for the next one or two hours? Because this is how much time it will take us to go through today's session."

"Yeah, but I'm going to work in sixty minutes…".

"Well, you'll need to postpone it then, because we must go through the whole workshop program that we have today! Otherwise, I would need to mark you today as - not attended - I hope you understand."

"Okay." sighs Larry and crosses his legs.

"Great, so, let's crack on then!" responds Aneke.

"By the way, what job do you do, Larry?"

"I work as a security guard in my friend's shop, he's from Taiwan, he sells gems, minerals, bracelets, chains, souvenirs, that kind of stuff. I keep people and goods on eye." responds the man feeling the vultures' penetrating stare.

"Cool." she says.

Larry grabs the watch on the table and checks the time, "Shit!" he whispers covering his mouth and rolls his eyes. It shows - 11:11.

There is a silence on the other side of the line, only interrupted by the sounds of a typewriter.

There's some noise in the corridor, someone is slamming the door and shouting "Tres, uno, dos." Then that crazy person shakes the door and repeats "Tres, uno, dos." and then runs away shouting "Go, go, go, go go…".

"What the fuck!" utters Larry.

"Sorry, what did you say? I'm just typing - logging our call…, sorry about keeping you waiting, Larry."

"No, it's fine, Aneke, there's just some mad person in the corridor."

"Oh, I see…".

Larry places the watch back on the table and picks the gun.

"So, I believe, there was an accident with your partner, wasn't it?" she starts.

"Ehm…well…I don't know…" he responds.

"Actually, is she your wife or partner? What is her name?"

"Her name is Rachel. She was my partner. We are separated now."

"And, what did you do to your ex, or what did you say?"

"I didn't do anything to her, I have never hurt anyone, I wouldn't harm a fly."

Larry plays with the gun.

"I see… But, why do you think the police have arrived and arrested you then?"

"I don't know, I was in shock! Because I didn't do anything. I didn't do anything to her nor to anyone else!"

"Yes, but there must have been some reason why the police were called…"

"I only took a piece of wood and smashed it against my friend's car. But I didn't break anything and the piece of wood got broken. That's all."

"So it was your friend?"

"Yeah, it used to be my best friend…".

"Then I took another piece of wood, some kind of wooden prism, and I used it to bang onto the door, onto the door of my own house, from which they did throw me away!"

"And why did you do that?"

"My best friend, he's twenty years older, he was coming for frequent visits, for a coffee, he was fooling my partner, he was trying to get her into the bed… I didn't know about that, Rachel told me. He was fooling her and making bad influences on her, putting myself into the bad light. You know he's twenty years older, he knows how to deal with young girls, if you know what I mean…"

"I see, and what happened next?"

"Then I looked through the small window above the main entrance door and there he was, coming downstairs, in his shorts, half naked, my best friend."

Larry angrily grabs a box of bullets from underneath the table and places it onto the table. The vulture's eye is closer, greener, more vigilant.

That mad someone in the corridor again shakes the door…

The siren of the fire truck goes off just a few blocks away, there's the Chinatown local fire station.

"Tres, dos, uno!"

The psychopath opens the door and closes it again slamming somewhere nearby outside in the corridor.

"Tres, dos, uno!"

The door shook noisily. And again. And once again.

"Go, go, go, go, goooooo!"

The noises of a running man.

Larry opens the small box and turns it upside down letting the bullets fall onto the glass table.

"And then, what happened after you saw your best friend in shorts…?" Aneke asks, trying to hide her hunger behind a neutral tone.

"You know, if you come to your house, after your girlfriend denies your call and doesn't come for the agreed meeting in town, after you see your best friend's car parking next to your house, and after you see your best friend in your house, through that small window above the door, running downstairs wearing just shorts… anyone would act like me… even you."

"What did you do after you saw your friend…?" Aneke repeats impatiently.

"Just please answer in one sentence and to the point. We have limited time for today's session." she adds.

"Okay." Larry nods.

Larry puts the hand gun onto the table, stands up and makes a few steps to the window. He adjusts the sun blinds to see properly what is going on in the street.

He can see his neighbour unloading a van, carrying some boxes into his house.

"So, then I banged onto the door, I wanted them to open it. They are lucky they didn't. If they did, it would be a fight, my best friend wouldn't be here anymore maybe… It would be brutal, I'm sure! Then I banged onto the window and it got broken. It was my own house! Yes it was written onto my partner's name, I did love Rachel so much, she was my whole life and my best friend did take everything away from me, my love, my Rachel and my house. He did fool her, then, now she regrets, he did start to abuse her, she had to escape! Once she had to hide from him under one car for one full hour!"

"I see…" Aneke says.

There is a moment of silence. Larry can hear Aneke typing on the other side of the telephone line. Larry moves from the window back and looks at the watch on the wall. It shows 11:45.

He walks to the kitchen and starts preparing a cup of coffee for himself.

Larry feels so tired and sleepy and needs to find a way to keep himself awake.

There's quite a mess in his kitchen. It's clear right from the get go as he enters it, that there's no woman's hand present in the flat.

He opens the wardrobe, grabs a bottle, pulls the cork out by his teeth and pours a generous bit of dark rum into the coffee in a monster-size mug.

"Sorry, I'm typing the notes…" the woman's voice on the phone says.

"That's alright, take your time…"

Larry sips a hot drink from the mug.

As he drinks the coffee with rum, he spots sandglass on the shelf.

"How long have you been with your partner, with Rachel I mean?"

"Nine years."

"Do you have any children?"

"No, not together, but she has brought five children from her previous relationship. But they have been taken away from her by the social services anyway. Rachel has got problems with alcohol… I've tried to help her, I fell in love with her, she was my life. I was taking care of her children as if they were my own. I didn't consider them to be strangers to me. And you know what, Aneke, they come to see Rachel's children from time to time. That pleases me a lot. They do not come to see their own mom Rachel but they come to see me instead. It's a great feeling, you know. I was changing their nappies, I was cooking for them, doing the homework with them. We've had a lot of fun together!" Larry gets emotional, grabs the sandglass and walks back to the living room.

"I'm sure it's a big satisfaction for you, Larry." the counsellor on the line says.

Larry makes a few more steps to the window and opens the sun blinds with his two fingers, letting the sun rays in.

"Yeah. It is, indeed. It always makes me happy when they come to see me."

"Yeah…" Aneke adds in an understanding tone.

Larry observes a few children, Chinese, Afroamerican, Latinos, all together, as they play with a football and scream. They are so full of energy, living only in the present time, as if they were on some powerful drug. What a contrast to Larry's physical and mental state. They don't think about the past because they barely have some and they don't think about the future, because there's a whole eternity ahead of them.

Larry raises his hand with the sandglass and holds it against the sun rays.

"*There's an Indian tribe somewhere in Amazonas, they live only in the present, there's no past, there's no future, there's no death, no dreams, no life, only NOW…*" he contemplates, "*…and they flow, their souls, like the river, without spring and without the sea…*".

A big car arrives with the loud bass speakers playing the known tune about "Time".

Larry's mind moves thousands miles away to the desert, he walks the dunes, it's hot and he comes to the edge of a cliff.

He stares down into the abyss observing the monstrous waves crashing against the rocks.

Larry is hypnotised, he stretches his hands and jumps.

At first, he's falling down and the deadly hit seems to be inevitable, but then he raises back up and flies over the sea towards the horizon.

An angel appears in the distance right before him.

The angel is a beautiful woman holding an old school telephone in her hand.

She says "And how is it now? What have been your reflections on that relationship, on that incident?".

Larry enters back "our reality" sitting back in his favourite armchair and holding the sandglass.

He positions it carefully onto the table and observes the tiny sand grains falling from the upper chamber down.

"Yea, now I don't think about anything… It's a question of the past. It has happened, yea, but it's all over. If I met my best friend, I would pay attention to him, I would just walk by without any thoughts, without any emotions. If I met my ex partner Rachel, I would say hi, she would say hi, we would maybe talk, but that would be it. It's over. It happened, yeah, but it's time to move on." Larry sounds firm, that he actually means what he says.

"That's great, Larry, I'm glad to hear that!" Aneke responds with a loud smile.

"Yeah, I did my best, she had my heart in the palm of her hand, Rachel. But, she did disappoint me, betray me, with my best friend. It might not be even her fault entirely, because my best friend - he's twenty years older and he's streetwise, smart, he knows how to deal with people, to gain what he desires.

That's the fact." the man contemplates into the phone.

The tune in the car radio outside changes.

There is a momentarily silence on the phone line.

Larry listens to it while Rachel on the other end of the phone line is typing.

In the meantime somewhere in China Town the people do their own stuff, some are locals, some visitors from the Chicago metropolitan area, some have arrived from Kansas, some from California. There are also the tourists who came from Europe or Africa, Asia or Australia, from Mexico and Philippines. There's also one gentleman from Czech Republic. Many Poles, few Russians, some Mormons, Moroccans, Jews, you name it.

The main attraction is the food, that's the magnet number one!

And one can smell it, the thousands of different smells, hitting you on every corner. There's no escape, you gotta have the dish or two or three.

Well, you can see the most big and fancy cars here, the Chinese in ChinaTown are rich. And that's why they need a ChinaTown Police - a kind of neighbourhood watch. They use the very same cars as the Chicago police do.

The gangs from south Chicago are coming here with no peaceful minds.

They shoot a person or more here and there over here, despite the precautions.

And that is one of the main reasons Larry lives here.

He was allocated to this district, to uncover the South Chicago gangs.

He came here as an undercover, on Harley Davidson, as a biker, heavily tattooed, sunbathed, with the stories about how he had suffered hardship during his imprisonment. He even deals the marijuana here, he's whole deal authentic. He works as a security guard in his Taiwanese friend's shop. He makes the chains and bracelets for the shop at his home. His profile here is impenetrable. No one ever suspected he could be a federal agent.

Larry is cool. He would never go to the police and told the police that some are laundering their dollars in the brothels, through the prostitution, night clubs. He's loyal to his friends here. His mission is different, he is after the South Chicago gangs who come here to murder and steal.

So these are the standings here for Larry, well, as long as the assignment and the responsibilities or duties attached to the job stay the same…

But, he would never use his friends' services, he didn't go with the girls, he was loyal to his partner Rachel. Unlike her. She has broken the bond by betraying him with his best friend!

"Larry, are you still there?"

The response is snoring!

"Larry?"

Larry's head partly rests on his arm and his eyes are closed.

"Larry!" shouts Aneke from the phone that has fallen down onto the carpet.

Snoring.

The window is little opened and the noise of the big city crawls inside as it becomes the dominant sound.

The sun rays paint geometric shadow patterns on the walls as the cars pass by and as the sun moves higher up in the sky.

The last sand grains are falling down in the sandglass.

The response to Aneke is dead silence interrupted by snoring.

Aneke is still trying to say something from the mobile phone on the floor, but

Larry makes the noises as he sleeps deep.

She hangs up.

It's pretty difficult to say what time of the day is. The heavy curtains are closed. They move and wave softly pushed by the soft breeze entering the room through the opened window.

The doctor said to Larry to keep warm, especially his hands, but also his back, face, knees, feet, the whole body and never to get exposed to the cold wind or freezing weather. But Larry never listens to others, he downplays everything, well not quite, as regarding his job of federal agent investigator, he's a smart and precise detective. He pays his attention to the smallest details, because as he frequently says, the devil is in the detail. Larry works on himself hard first, he joins the ChinaTown local Kung Fu club at St. Archer Avenue, he exercises everyday in the Sun Yet-San Playground Park. But lately, he suffers with occasional pain and spasm in his hands and fingers, sometimes in his knees too. His thumbs are getting black and knees and ankles are getting blueish. Sometimes when he walks his body becomes stiff, his mouth - lips are affected, his speech gets awkward, the veins all over his body stretch and he loses control -

balance and falls down. He has found out that immersing his body into the hot water helps him almost instantly. Then he needs to wear proper clothes covering his whole body, protecting him from the wind.

Even during summer he wears a winter hat, or any hat, like trapper hat, beane, baseball hat, cowboy hat and even a deer stalker or yellow hard hat. He likes to impersonate, he likes change, he wants to be different maybe, he's a man of many hats. Larry enjoys pretending to be someone he's not. If he wasn't a detective, he would almost certainly be an actor. Usually he wears a long raincoat falling down to his feet, the one you can see in the Spaghetti Westerns, damn long, well worn and so cool. He's kind of the good guy with bad manners and jokes, he enjoys helping people in need and he appreciates making them smile or better laugh. Because as he frequently says, a day without laughter is the lost day.

His doctor has diagnosed him with rheumatoid osteoarthritis and prescribed Steroids to treat the conditions in general and Naproxen as a mild to moderate painkiller. The corticosteroids come in the form of injections and are anti-inflammatory injections and the Naproxen are the pills. As a last resort - Larry found himself some Codeine in tablets and Morphine in capsules and liquid. The unfortunate prognosis of Dr. Ben is, it will get only worse and there will be time, when even the softest wind will drive Larry insane. Managing the pain will become Larry's main objective as time will go by. But now, he's still got some time to fix the things that are important stuff in life. His name is Larry Fixman.

His visits to the Sun Yet-San Playground park, where the locals enjoy playing Chinese chess and the kids rampage on a swing, are less frequent, only on sunny warm windless days. His Harley Davidson and obsolete car stay parked idle and the rust starts to make its way. He comes to the park to do Tai-Chi and Kung Fu exercises, sometimes he plays chess with his friends and sometimes he just sits in the swing wearing one of his hats and the damn long well worn rain coat, enjoying his "always-last-cigarette", coffee and red bean bun.

He's got a plenty of time to contemplate, because his job is to be someone else, someone - who has all the time of the world, someone who's a local fixer, the good neighbour, neighbourhood watch man, retired biker doing the evening shifts in his Taiwanese friend's store, Vietnamese war veteran, divorced, single and so cool. His job is to merge with this community, listen very well and foresee the crimes to stop the bad guys from making them happen.

No one has ever suspected he would be an FBI guy.

"That funny kind-hearted Larry? Never!"

Larry would do many things in life differently, he has made many mistakes, especially in his relationships with people, people who were close to him, he did hurt them the most. He was able to fix the strangers' problems - here and there, but he did struggle in his own life. Perhaps he got easily lost in the challenges of the others, maybe he had played too much poker and lost too much money, or it could be that had simply never focused on what was the most important thing in each particular moment of his life...

Yes, intuition Larry masters is handy to solve the crimes, to deal with thugs, to uncover the hyenas, or survive in the federal bureau agency mind puzzle labyrinth - but in real life, what is crucial, is the patient organisation towards common goal. Let's say, for example, between two partners, honest communication, planning together and sticking to the goal no matter what black cat crosses your road! Loyalty and mutual support...

That's the way to pass the test in life.

It's that simple, it doesn't have to always finish well, because there are the circumstances, health and luck in the game too, but as long as we stick to the rules of cool partnership, we'll get the high score.

It's that simple, not easy, it's the long journey full of hardship, it's worth it.

It's a great way!

There's a bust statue in the Sun Yet-San Playground Park.

The eyes of the bronze head sitting on the granite block stare at the Willis Tower that was the world's tallest building upon completion in 1974 until 1998. The tower is known also as the Sears Tower and it dominates the Chicago Downtown.

That bronze head belongs to Dr. Sun Yet-San, of course, "The Father of The Republic of China" and there on the granite block is engraved the following exact text:

*When the Great Way is implemented, the world-state is for the equality of
all the peoples. The sagacious and capable are appointed as civilian officials.
Trustworthiness is instilled and neighbourliness cultivated.
Therefore, people are pious to all parents, not just their own parents,
nurture all children, not just their own children. The old are provided
for till their death, the adults are employed, and the young developed.
Widows and widowers, orphans and the childless, the sick
and disabled, all are well cared for. Men have their proper positions,
women have their families. Wasting of commodities are despised, nor
hoarding them for their own use. Not contributing one's efforts are
abhorred, same as devoting them for one's own ends.
Thus, evil schemes are repressed and cannot flourish; robbers, thieves,
and rebels cannot commit their crimes. Therefore, doors do not need to be
closed, this is called "the Age of Great Comity"*

*Presented by:
District 300 of Lions international,
The Republic of China*

*Reconstruction in 2018 by:
Overseas Community Affairs Council
The Republic of China
Chinese Consolidated Benevolent Association of Chicago*

Larry keeps repairing his disable friend's small pocket radio.

His friend Johny Milano, called by his friends the Captain, lost his legs in the mafia crossfire. Johny claims it was the blast of a grenade.

Johnny has long white hair, he looks like an Italian Indian, he wears thick fake gold chains and white undershirt, he is in a wheelchair.

People can always find him on the same corner during hot summer afternoons.

Larry is disrupted by some noise from behind the wall or somewhere from the corridor.

He stops in what he was doing and listens.

The bed scratching the floor, loud sighs, the sighs of pleasure…

Larry listens to it and a miracle paints a soft cheeky smile on his face.

Nevertheless, that couple gets even louder, wild, or maybe it's some threesome, double or gang…?

Larry grabs a pair of earphones, sticks them into his ears, finds some tune on his mobile, switches the bluetooth on and forgets the furious bangers.

It's a Polish tune, hip-hop. Larry's ancestors come from Poland and he was born and raised in Chicago - Schaumburg: *"Next time…, make sure they're all dead before you leave…"*

Larry gets back to work on Johny's radio, he's perplexed, he knows how to destroy radios, not how to repair them. When he was three years old, his father did land him a radio not to leave alone as he headed for work.

It was a fancy top quality radio, bigger than small Larry and his father had to do some nasty hours working in steel works. When his father returned back home, exhausted and thirsty, he had found his radio dismantled to the smallest parts.

"I think, I'll better buy the new one for Johny…" mumbles Larry in his mind frustrated.

He throws the micro screwdriver across the table "Fuck that!"

He sits, stars at the waving curtain and rubs his hands with a painful grimace.

Larry stands up and takes a few steps to the window, closes it and as he turns he stumbles a bit almost falling down to the floor.

He observes the palms of his hands as the fingers begin twisting and the veins all over his body tighten. The man runs to the bathroom and turns on the hot water tap all the way through and then opens a cold water tap a bit to make a bearable melange - the bath. Then he quickly opens the mirror wardrobe and grabs a bag and medications, he sits on the toilet and opens the bag. There are syringes ready filled with corticosteroids, he picks one and it almost falls onto the wet tiles and his fingers refuse to listen to him. He gathers all his strength and with a pain in his face he injects it into a muscle on his heavily tattooed hand - right into the eye hole of skull. He drops the bag that in a slow motion falls onto the floor. He takes a small plastic bottle with a sigh: "*Morphin*" and crawls to the bathtub. The next minute he dives into the hot water and opens the bottle, picks one capsule and swallows it.

He immerses his hands slowly into the hot water and closes his eyes as the vapour rises up bedewing the mirrors. He falls into a micro-sleep.

He has a strange dream about a blue swirl in the sky.

That blue hypnotic pattern keeps turning and magnetises Larry.

Or it is moving closer and closer towards the man or he is levitating towards the swirl. It seems there's a face of a beautiful woman in the centre of that swirl! Is she an angel? But her face is serious...

He never knew the angels are that serious...

He can hear some noises - as if someone was tuning the radio.

And then, he hears a ringtone - the mobile ringtone. The familiar one.

Larry opens his eyes and tries to orientate in space and time.

His mobile phone keeps ringing.

It's on the floor on the carpet.

He bends with a bad mood and sighs, he touches the green vibrating circle with a phone pictogram.

"Hello...who's that?"

"It's Aneke!"

"Aneke who?" Larry utters still sleepy, besotted.

"Aneke from Partnership Solution Charity in Durham! What has happened, Larry?" I heard snoring!"

"Oh, yea, I'm sorry, please take my apologies! I was last night at work, I was so tired, I fell asleep... Oh, I must have fallen asleep, I guess."

"Larry, if you won't pay attention to our workshop, if you'll sleep while I'm talking, we'll need to finish this session and I would need to report it to the police - as not attended. Do you hear me?" she says angrily.

"Yes, ma'm, I'm sorry, I was so tired."

"This workshop is for your good. And, above all, this was released by the authorities as a part of conditional caution… You don't want the police arriving at your doorstep again, do you?!"

"No, I don't."

"Good!"

"So, let's continue, because we have a limited time, Larry!"

"Yea."

"You know, they were behaving really violently, those three cops, they were three of them I think. They were shouting at me to keep my hands up, they jumped on me and put me onto the ground, like crazy, I have never hurt anyone, I don't have any criminal record and they behaved like mad! Even the neighbour went down, especially when they saw that he did record everything on camera, she said to the police that they cannot behave like that! And you know what, they started to behave normal to me, when they realised I can communicate with them. And the next day? They came for her - my neighbour who had recorded everything - they took her with them to the police custody. Unbelievable…" Larry becomes emotional.

But Aneke interrupts "If you want to raise a complaint, you have all the legal rights to do so. There's a strict procedure, you can fill the form online, you can report it or take it to the court. We don't have time to discuss that today and I'm from the charity, I've nothing to do with the police."

"Okay." Larry responds.

Larry is now vigilant and he tries to recall the series of his strange dreams.

He has been always writing his dreams down and trying to analyse them.

Frequently he used his dreams, daydreams and intuition to solve crimes, cases, but if he did use them also for his own good and the good of people who are close to him, he would do even better.

He stands up and walks to a chest of drawers and pulls them one by one in a search for something that strikes his mind out of a sudden.

"We're now getting into a second stage of our initial workshop, Larry."

"Yes."

"There's a city in North America called Duluth." she says and makes a brief pause. Then Aneke continues.

"They did a special research in that city in the 1980s. And, as a result of that extensive research they have developed The Power and Control Wheel, which is a tool that helps explain different ways an abusive partner can use power and control to manipulate a relationship. This program - The Duluth Model (also known as DAIP - Domestic Abuse Intervention Project) - was developed to reduce domestic violence against women. This program was mostly sponsored by feminist Ellen Pence. The Power and Control Wheel makes the pattern, intent and impact of violence visible. Are you with me, Larry?"

"Yes, listening…" Larry responds.

"Wonderful!" she says and continues.

"As I said already, there are different ways an abusive partner can use power and control to manipulate a relationship and we'll go one by one. The first one - USING INTIMIDATION - to keep the victim fearful.

Another strategy is "ISOLATION", which means controlling when the victim can leave the home. Some bullies in the household use "ECONOMIC ABUSE", to deny the victim access to money. Or perhaps the "COERCION" and threats, like convincing the victim to do something illegal. Very tricky and rude one is especially "EMOTIONAL ABUSE" like degrading the victim.

Some bad guys pick the "MALE PRIVILEGE", to define men's and women's roles. Some are using the "CHILDREN, including threatening to file for custody if the survivor leaves. And then, we also have this strategy - minimising, denying and blaming, such as "GASLIGHTING".

Nevertheless, the abuse is not limited only to the aforementioned strategies, the much worse is the physical violence and sexual abuse, I mean not only physical sexual abuse but also the psychological sexual abuse. This means for example sexist or pervert remarks that make the victim feel abused, humiliated or cornered." Aneke pauses.

"I just hope you're not sleeping again, Larry, are you?!"

"No. no, listening…". He answers.

"You know, it's all the mind game." She says.

"So, tell me, can you identify any of those strategies that led to that "INCIDENT" between you and your ex-partner."

"I didn't do any of that! I did love her so much." The man adds.

"Nothing has happened between me and Rachel, nothing of what you have mentioned, it was between me and my best friend."

"Alright, I think it was the INTIMIDATION, because you were using force, breaking things, making the victim fearful." Aneke says.

"It was not pointed out to Rachel, I was raging, because my best friend did what he did, they did betray me… How about you? What would you do, if that happened to you, if you found your husband in bed with your best friend? Both of them are having a good time… " Larry strikes back.

The man smiles, because he knows the score, *people tell people how they should lead their life and at the same time they struggle to keep it together themselves…*

People can be pretty toxic too! And it is better to stay away from toxic people at all costs. Often they have honey-like voices, but they spill the poison. Larry feels the officer or the psychology adviser on the other side just

"Well, it's not about me, I'm here to lead the seminar, to educate you on domestic violence abuse to make sure we don't meet again!"

"Okay, okay…" Larry utters in a surrender of the escapist.

Larry becomes impatient, *this all is taking way too long!*

He grabs that broken radio and the repair tools as he is on the call.

Aneke talks and talks and Larry tries to fix the device for his friend.

The woman's talking merges into a kind of incomprehensible murmur in the background as the heat in the room rises.

The man is sweating but finally finds what was wrong with the thing! But it still requires a lot of work.

A few hours later

Larry still struggles to repair the old radio. In fact, it seems he did dismantle it into the tiniest pieces. He sits in the swinging chair and listens to the raging storm as the night crawls to the ChinaTown in Windy City.

He swings and his mind is totally empty.

Out of the blue, the rain and thunder are disrupted by a familiar noise from the corridor.

That lunatic is slamming the door and shouting again "Tres, uno, dos." Then the mad person shakes the door and repeats "Tres, uno, dos." and then runs away shouting "Go, go, go, go go…".

"Oh my God!" whispers Larry ominously.

The man in the swinging chair grabs a handgun from the shelf and a box of bullets.

Again "Tres, uno, dos."

Larry loads the gun and gazes at the antique radio.

"Tres, uno, dos."

Larry stops swinging in the chair and empties the colt magazine into the radio.

The radio has broken into the pieces, but yet some part of it stands still untouched.

The gust of wind opens the window wide and the raindrops hit Larry's face.

The flashes in the sky light the buildings on the other side of the street and the loudest thunder ever follows shortly after that.

Bang!

The light in the room goes off as the electricity in the area is gone.

Bang!

Another lightning just a few blocks away and a scary thunder slams man's ears.

Silence and darkness is now interrupted only by soft rain.

As the rain decreases in its intensity and the window calms down temporarily, something unexpected happens …

A blue shining ball enters the room and stays there for a moment levitating in the air.

Larry is in shock and freezes for a moment.

"*Ball lightning!*" comes to his mind.

He points his colt at the thing.

Cocks the gun.

Click. The magazine is empty.

The blue shining ball starts moving slowly towards the radio and enters one of its bulbs that spreads an intensive light in the room.

Crackling sound comes out of that radio bulb and gradually increases in its volume.

Larry is unable to move in the chair.

And then, something very strange happens!

The radio seems to be tuning itself on its own through the frequencies as if it was searching for some cool radio station.

"Hello …" the voice strikes Larry out of the radio remnants.

"Hello, is anybody there?" the voice of a young boy comes out of the shining bulb again.

Larry stares at the bulb.

"Please, help!" radio whispers with its obscured antique sound.

Larry leans forward.

"Hey there … Who are you?" Larry asks.

"Oh, hi, hi! Thanks to Delissmen! Hi!" the radio answers.

"Where are you?" The man in the swinging chair leans closer to the bulb covering his eyes from the overwhelming light.

"This is Andrew, from Beach Town, we need help!"

"What happened?" Larry asks.

"The Mayor, our city mayor is killing people, torturing them!"

"What?"

"Where's the Beach Town?"

"Yesterday, they found another few bodies on the beach, they were buried in the dunes … They were slaughtered, like …, as if some monster did bite their necks and tear their spinal cords off their backs …, but I know, it's the Mayor Sinister behind those awful ugly crimes!"

"Mayor who?" Larry frowns and shakes his head.

"Mayor Will Sinister!"

"Please come, come to help us, otherwise we're all gonna die, the Mayor got insane!"

"Listen, I'm a cop, or … sort of …" Larry mumbles.

"But, how to hell, do you call me through my radio?'

"What's that?" the voice on the other side wonders.

"Listen, boy, where are you?"

"I told you already, in the Beach Town!"

"How did you get to me?" Larry shouts, because the rain and thunder are coming back.

"Through the Teleufonium." the boy answers.

"Whats that?"

"I have developed it, it's a special device and with it I can penetrate the Mayor's communication shield.'

"Teleufonium?"

"Yeah."

"Where's the Beach Town?" Larry insists on getting the answer.

"It's somewhere between Grand Diego and Dijuana in Sunnyfornia …".

"What? You mean in California, no?!"

"Sunnyfornia." the boy repeats.

Bang!

Thunder.

Larry shakes his head.

Bang! Another one.

"Listen Andrew, stop this bullshit, I've never heard of Grand Diego or Sunnyfornia …" Larry shouts in a pointless attempt to drown the series of epic thunders.

Bang!!

The flash of the lightning just behind the window lits the room white and a brutally loud thunder grasps Larry's place into a firm life squeezing fist.

Larry loses his consciousness.

And when he wakes up, there's a morning, sunrise, birds singing …

Larry is on the ground, he tries to sit down and touches his head.

It must have been just a dream.

But his hand touches something on the carpet.

He grabs it and raises it before his eyes.

The blurry vision turns gradually into a sharp sight.

He holds a radio bulb in his hand.

Teleufonium.

TANEZCOR PICTURES LLC & INTERNATIONAL INVESTORS PRESENT
OMAR ZAHID'S
SWITCHER STRIKES

*Someone you can trust is worth more than all
the material treasures in the world...*